The National Museum
of Capodimonte

first floor

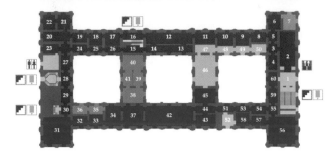

2 to 30
Farnese Gallery
Italian and foreign paintings
15th - 17th centuries
Gallery of rare objects (*rooms 13-14*)

7
Borgia Collection
Paintings and objects
of Western and Eastern art
12th - 18th centuries

23 31 to 60
Royal Apartments
Paintings, sculptures, furnishing
and the decorative arts
18th - 19th centuries

35 36
Gallery of porcelain ware

46 to 50
Farnese and Bourbon Armoury

52
Porcelain Salottino

38 to 40
de Ciccio Collection
Paintings, sculptures and decorative arts
Western and Eastern
13th - 18th centuries

mezzanine floor
Cabinet of drawings and prints

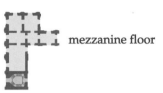

mezzanine floor

second floor

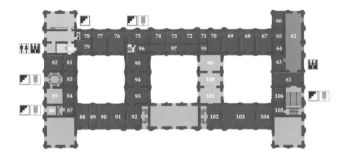

61 to 106
Gallery of the Arts in Naples
from the 1200s to the 1700s
Paintings and sculptures
13th - 16th centuries (*rooms 61-77*)
17th century (*rooms 78-98 and 102-103*)
18th century (*rooms 104-106*)

99 to 101
d'Avalos Collection

62
Gallery of the d'Avalos Tapestries

Contemporary art

third floor

Contemporary art

Section of photographs by Mimmo Jodice

Gallery for exhibition of modern
and contemporary art

Soprintendenza per i Beni
Artistici e Storici di Napoli

Edited by Nicola Spinosa

whith the contribution of
Luisa Ambrosio, Umberto Bile,
Pierluigi Leone de Castris,
Linda Martino, Mariaserena Mormone,
Rossana Muzii, Mariella Utili

photographs by
Ugo Pons Salabelle and Luigi Di Maggio

The National Museum
of Capodimonte

Electa Napoli

Electa Napoli

Editing
Silvia Cassani

Graphic design and layout
Enrica D'Aguanno
Nadia Bronzuto

Translation
Philip Sands
Gabriella Granata
Sara Carcatella

Photographs
Pages 44, 97, 99: Bruno Arciprete
Page 118: Gaeta & Gaeta
Pages 22, 55, 67, 72, 101, 120, 135, 144, 145, 245, 247: Archivio dell'Arte - Luciano Pedicini
Pages 43, 87, 90, 91, 183, 197, 199, 202, 232, 23 above, 251, 269: Soprintendenza Speciale per il Polo Museale Napoletano

The texts from p. 19 to 102 are by Pierluigi Leone de Castris; from p. 105 to 148 by Mariella Utili; from p. 151 to 189 by Mariaserena Mormone; from p. 193 to 218 by Rossana Muzii; from p. 221 to 293 by Luisa Ambrosio and Linda Martino; from p. 295 to 300 by Umberto Bile

Printed in Italy
First English edition September 1996
© Copyright 2003 by **Ministero per i Beni e le Attività Culturali**
Soprintendenza Speciale
per il Polo Museale Napoletano
electa napoli srl
Gruppo Mondadori Electa S.p.A.
Second reprint June 2003

Contents

The National Museum of Capodimonte

The origins of the Museum of Capodimonte could be said to almost coincide with the historical and dynastic events which, at the end of the Polish war of succession in 1734, brought to the throne of Naples, Charles of Bourbon, Duke of Parma and Piacenza. He was the son of Philip V of Spain and Elisabetta Farnese, last descendant of a powerful and ancient family which prospered in Italy and Europe half-way through the 16th century. Charles inherited, from his mother, the Farnese collection which consisted of paintings, drawings, bronzes, artistic objects, furniture, medals and coins, jewels, cameos and archaeological finds. Charles decided to unify the collection, until then scattered in various palaces (Palazzo della Pilotta and Palazzo del Giardino in Parma, Palazzo Ducale in Piacenza, the Residence of Colorno and Palazzo Farnese in Rome), and to transfer it to Naples.

The vast collection was initially concentrated in the ancient Royal Palace in the centre of the city. Part of it was lodged in some rooms on the piano nobile, another part in containers distributed along the staircase and in the entrance halls on the ground-floor. Everything was in such a shameful state of abandon that the Frenchman de Brosses, who saw the collection between 1739 and 1740, recorded how some famous paintings were still left in cases.

However, Charles of Bourbon and his ministers had already decided to have a new Royal Palace built in order to house the most important parts of the collection. The place chosen was the hill of Capodimonte, on the edge of a wood, in an attractive position facing west and overlooking the Gulf of Naples. Vast quantities of land were confiscated for the Palace and the project was entrusted to the military engineer Giovanni Antonio Medrano from Palermo, who was assisted, for a short time, by the more expert Roman architect, Antonio Canevari.

Medrano drew up three distinct projects for the Capodimonte residence. The project which was finally chosen foresaw the construction of a vast rectangular building (170 metres long and 87 wide), with only a mezzanine, two floors and the attics. The building, once constructed, stretched imposingly in the longitudinal sense and was broken up by three large, porticoed, inter-communicating courtyards opening outwards through wide arches. With regard to the exterior, the Palace had austere façades in Doric style (considered the most apt for a building which had to host a museum) and neo-cinquecento mood. The front facing façade was highlighted by the contrast between the strong framework in grey 'piperno' (a kind of eruptive rock) with the typical red of the Neapolitan plastered walls, and also by a succession of tall windows on the piano nobile with smaller openings on the other floors. On the piano nobile, the interior of the building was a monotonous, interminable succession of rooms which were destined for official receptions, royal apartments and for the exhibition of the Farnese collection. This succession of rooms was interrupted by a wide gallery of twice the normal height and, at the corners of the palace, by reception rooms which were also of twice the height of the other minor rooms. The service areas and the servants' lodgings occupied more modest space on the ground floor, on the mezzanine and on the second floor. The layout of the piano nobile, as it is today, is profoundly different from its original plan. There have been, over the years, various modifications due to changing tastes and to the different uses of the building during the last century and after the end of the second World War.

On the 9th September 1738, the foundation stone was solemnly laid and the work began, under the direction of the previously mentioned Medrano. The contract was given to the royal building contractor, Angelo Carasale, later arrested for profiteering. During the first months the construction of the building proceeded rapidly. Tufaceus stones, obtained from excavations made for the deep foundations of the building, were used, overcoming the many obstacles caused by the transport of the material to the hill of Capodimonte, which was to be reached only by means of a steep, uphill climb. Hence, the cavities – which were created as a consequence – were then used as ample cisterns indispensable because of the chronic lack of water. At the beginning of 1739, a board of experts decided that those rooms facing south and towards the sea – less prone to damp and with the best light – were to be reserved for the paintings, whilst the so called 'back rooms', which faced onto the wood, had been set apart for books, medals and other objects. Between 1742 and 1743, work had started on a park and gardens in the area around the Royal Palace which was still under construction. These had been planned by the Neapolitan architect Ferdinando Sanfelice, to whom in the same year, 1743, the planning of the building for the Royal Porcelain Factory of Capodimonte had also been entrusted. Sanfelice's plan for the park, only partially carried out, provided for the creation of a scenic setting clearly influenced by the baroque style, with five, long tree-lined avenues, radiating from the entrance square. The plan included the introduction of numerous marble statues and the visually inpressive intersection of minor avenues coming out of the dense natural undergrowth, scattered plants and scented herbs. The idea was to link the traditional taste for the symmetrically ordered Italian garden, re-adapted on French lines, with the more modern Romantic tendency for the apparently spontaneous English garden. But the work was interrupted and only in 1766 did the architect Ferdinando Fuga resume and finish part of the project introducing some changes.

Very soon though, the work on the Royal Palace slowed down noticeably, not only on account of technical difficulties but also because of the heavy expenses involved. For the work at Portici and Capodimonte the Royal Treasury was forced to pay out up to 5,000 ducats a month, until the end of 1759. Furthermore, the probable loss of interest on the sovereign's part also played a role, as since 1751 he had been interested in the events connected with the construction of the new Palace of Caserta, in line with Luigi Vanvitelli's plan. Therefore, on the 1st February 1758, 20 years after the approval of the plan, work on the northern side had not yet been started and only 12 of the 24 rooms making up the piano nobile, had been completed. These were the rooms set aside for the library, the medal room, the picture gallery and for the collection of antiques brought from Casa Farnese in Parma. The paintings were mounted in September of the following year, under the direction of padre Giovan Maria della Torre. The final arrangement was completed only in 1764, when Charles of Bourbon had already been on the throne of Madrid for five years and many foreign visitors had already come to visit some of the rooms of the new Royal Museum of Capodimonte.

In 1758, in fact, Winckelmann visited the Royal Palace and, although mainly interested in the collection of medals and coins, was favourably impressed by some paintings from the Farnese Picture Gallery, sufficiently so to compare it in importance with the more famous Dresden Gallery. In 1761 Fragonard, following on Saint-Non, arrived in Naples where he made sketches of some of the most famous paintings on show and later had them engraved and printed for the *Voyage pittoresque*, published in Paris in 1781. In 1763 the young Angelika Kauffmann came to study at Capodimonte. Also Canova came in the February of 1780 when he recorded the presence of a small menagerie in the neighbouring wood with wild beasts and other exotic animals. In 1787 Goethe complained about the general lack of order in the exhibition, although he praised the presence in the Royal Palace of a large number of highly valuable works. Unfortunately, since the original inventory compiled in 1756 by the painter Clemente Ruta of Parma had been destroyed and no catalogue, even of the picture gallery itself, had ever been printed, we have practically no knowledge either of the effective size of the collection, or of the criteria adopted by padre della Torre. Therefore, we can only conclude – from brief quotations by Lalande in 1765-66 and by Sigismondo in 1788-89, or from the travel notes of 1783 by Tommaso Puccini, later director of the Uffizi – that the essential structure of Capodimonte consisted of a succession of rooms facing south, where the Farnese paintings were displayed and grouped according to the individual artists or to the regional schools of art. In the wing facing the park, six rooms had been allotted to the library, one to the medal collection, a few others to a section showing natural history exhibits and others to the collection of small bronze figures, cameos, carved gems and various antiques.

In 1759 Ferdinand IV came to the throne with Bernardo Tanucci as regent. Between 1761-1765 the royal apartments were joined to the wing destined for the Farnese museum by several rooms and two galleries, later to be used as a ballroom and exhibition area for the armoury. In 1787 the German artist Federico Anders, called from Rome, started a systematic restoration of a large number of paintings which needed urgent attention. The number continued to grow because the canvases which had decorated the Cloakroom of Palazzo Farnese in Rome were transferred to Capodimonte and several pictures, both from the Neapolitan School and from other Southern schools were purchased by the sovereign (some oil on panels by Cesare da Sesto and Polidoro da Caravaggio which came from Messina, and canvases by Ribera, Stomer and Giordano from Neapolitan churches and convents). So that, before the French plundered the Museum in 1799, the paintings present in Capodimonte had increased to no less than the 1,783 items listed in the inventory.

In 1798, Ferdinand IV – fearing that the Jacobin and anti-Bourbon uprisings could spread to Naples – moved to Palermo, taking with him, from Capodimonte, fourteen pictures and the whole Farnese Library. One year later the French troops, commanded by General Championnet, carried a large number of paintings away from the Royal Palace. A number of these pictures were later recovered in Rome, in San Luigi dei Francesi and elsewhere, and were put together with some excellent purchases made by Domenico Venuti. However, this part of the collection, also increased by some donations, was not returned to Capodimonte but was arranged in 1801 in the palace of the Prince of Altavilla, outside the gate of Chiaja, which had for some time been rented by the Court as an occasional Royal residence. Here, within a short period, a famous picture gallery was created which included many other paintings of different origin. The Sovereign had planned to house this collection, besides the ones still on show in Capodimonte, with the famous collections of antiques kept in the Palazzo Farnese in Rome and the ever growing collection of archaeological findings coming from the excavations of Pompeii and Herculaneum. These findings were temporarily arranged in the Royal Palace of Portici and in the 17th century Palazzo dei Regi Studi at Foria. Ferdinando Fuga and later Pompeo Schiantarelli were to convert Palazzo dei Regi Studi into a great museum that would house the Farnese and the Bourbon collections.

The plan was blocked because of the victorious advance of the Napoleonic troops in 1806 which forced the King to flee to Palermo with the Court. This time he took 66 paintings, together with various pieces of furniture taken from Capodimonte and the Francavilla Palace. The project was resumed by the French Administration after the formation of the Napoleonic kingdom, with first Giuseppe Bonaparte and later, in 1808, Joachim Murat. They added to the already existing collections, numerous paintings acquired through the suppression of monasteries in Naples and other southern regions. Their aim was that of creating a National Gallery as part of the new museum capable of documenting fully the evolution of the Neapolitan School of Art from its origin to the present day. In addition, Joachim Murat himself began to negotiate the purchase of archaeological, medieval, modern, eastern and western art collections, put together by Cardinal Stefano Borgia in the so called Velletri Museum. Thus, a new kind of museum was to be created in Naples, on the lines of the Louvre in Paris, the British Museum in London and the Altes of Berlin. In other words, a great universal museum that would house and display different artistic material, and that would represent the various and most important artistic trends matured over the centuries, in the East and in the West, in Italy and the rest of Europe. This programme was only completed when Ferdinand IV of Bourbon (Ferdinand I of the Two Sicilies) came back to Naples in 1815. Then, in the re-adapted Palazzo dei Regi Studi, the Royal Bourbon Museum was created. The museum gathered together the following: all the Farnese collections housed in Capodimonte or in the Altavilla Palace; the Archaeological collections from Palazzo Farnese in Rome; the archaeological findings of Pompeii and Herculaneum; Stefano Borgia's collection purchased in 1817; all the paintings from the suppressed monasteries. The only exception were the paintings and pieces of furniture that Ferdinand had taken with him to Palermo, and which he left in that city as a token of gratitude for the hospitality he had been offered. The vast collection of canvases and panels, increased through purchases (the paintings sold by the famous superintendent of the San Carlo Theatre, Barbaia, to the museum, in 1841) and successive private and Royal donations, made up a vast picture gallery inside the Museum which was subdivided into schools and epochs with printed catalogues, and organised according to prevailing pedagogic criteria. Unfortunately, in 1854, the private collection of Leopold of Bourbon, Prince of Salerno (Francesco I's brother), which included several Farnese paintings today exhibited at the Museum Condé at Chantilly, was sold. Nevertheless, in 1860, on the eve of the passing of the property of the Southern Kingdom over to the House of Savoy, the Picture Gallery of the Royal Bourbon Museum, shortly to be called the National Museum (a title it kept until 1957) was divided into 16 display rooms and had over 900 paintings on show. This number was reduced to slightly less than 800 after the Unification of Italy.

In the meantime, the Royal Palace of Capodimonte had become the habitual court residence. It was, by then, easier to reach, thanks to the construction between 1807 and 1809 of a bridge passing over the underlying quarter of the Sanità, and to the opening of the Corso Napoleone (the present Corso Amedeo d'Aosta). This was completed in 1824, with a monumental staircase designed by Antonio Niccolini, decorated with valuable ornaments which had come straight from Paris. In 1833, the work to complete the northern side of the building was resumed. In 1835 the main staircase was finally completed according to a plan drawn up by Tommaso Giordano together with the great hexagonal staircase on the southern side, probably designed in 1823 by Antonio Niccolini. Between 1836 and 1838 the principal reception rooms of the Palace (the Ballroom) were decorated in tempera colours by Salvatore Giusti, Giuseppe Marocco and other minor local decorators, and were embellished with marble fireplaces designed by Niccolini, and with various bronze candlesticks designed by Tito Angelini. When the work was finished, most of the Palace was occupied by the apartments of the various members of the Royal family and by illustrious guests. This is the wing which once used to house the paintings of those young Neapolitan artists sent to study in Rome with a 'crown grant'. In the surrounding park a vast project to transform the wood and the surrounding arable land into an English garden was started under the direction of the head gardener of the Royal Botanical Gardens, a German named Federico Dehenhardt. It involved that area left untouched by Sanfelice's previous work.

In 1860 the Royal Palace of Capodimonte was handed over to the Savoy family, and the collections were reorganised by Annibale Sacco, the Administrative Director of the Royal House. He took into consideration an already existing Bourbon plan for the creation of a modern Gallery of Art on the piano nobile. This was to be made up firstly of paintings of the early 19th century already mounted in the Royal apartments or in the adjoining rooms, that is, the large canvases by Camuccini and by Benvenuti destined for the Royal Palace of Caserta. The collection would also include academic canvases, chosen from other former Bourbon residences, and works of art purchased directly from numerous contemporary artists, chiefly Neapolitan. The work was started as early as 1864, and by 1884 the collection amounted to 605 paintings and 95 sculptures. In 1864 the Royal Armoury was also moved to the first floor at Capodimonte. It consisted of numerous and often priceless coats-of-armour and bayonets as well as fire-arms from either the Farnese (some were originally of the Medici's) or the Bourbon collection, which had long been abandoned in a few rooms on the ground floor of the Royal Palace of Naples. In 1866, when the Royal Palace of Portici became state property, the boudoir in polychrome porcelain was transferred to a room on the piano nobile of the Capodimonte Palace. The boudoir had been made for Queen Maria Amalia by Giuseppe Gricci half-way through the 18th century and decorated with refined taste after the manner of the chinoiseries. In 1873, Sacco transferred there all the porcelain objects and biscuit which still existed in the other former Bourbon residences, together with tapestries of the Royal Factory of San Carlo alle Mortelle and numerous other pieces of furniture whose original location is often unknown. In 1877 the floor, discovered in 1788 during the excavations made in an ancient Roman villa at Capri and restored, was transferred to the so called 'cradle room' in Capodimonte.

The Royal Palace was by now used by the new Italian sovereign and by various members of the House of Savoy for brief stays. Towards the end of the century the whole family of the Duca d'Aosta established itself there. In 1920, the Palace became state property and was handed over to the Administration of the Fine Arts, to be used in part as a museum open to the public. However, the Royal family continued to stay there until immediately after the Second World War.

In 1948, the urgent problem of finding an adequate building to house the Picture Gallery, at that time confined to a few rooms on the second floor of the National Museum, had to be faced. This necessity had often been voiced by people like Benedetto Croce (who first expressed his opinion in 1886 and again in 1902) as well as by other members of the world of culture and art. The Gallery had been progressively despoiled of its paintings from the very beginning of the Unification of Italy. Many of these paintings were of Farnese origin. Of the 329 pictures listed in 1708 and housed in the Garden Palace at Parma, only 186 have been traced to date, 136 in various Neapolitan museums and 50 scattered in different collections and sites in Italy and abroad. This spoliation concerned not only the Picture Gallery but also the former Bourbon residences which, in passing to the House of Savoy, were deprived of ornaments and furniture then used to decorate the institutional seats and prestigious offices of the Capital (the Quirinale, the Palace of Montecitorio, Palazzo Madama, Palazzo Chigi, Palazzo della Farnesina among others) and the new ministerial Roman offices abroad. One of the many examples is the 13 paintings sent in 1917 to St. Petersburg, then considered lost, and only lately recovered from the Embassy in Moscow. They were also used to decorate Prefect's offices (Prefetture), barracks and churches in Campania or elsewhere in the national territory, and even to be integrated with the collection of the new National Gallery of Modern Art in Rome. Even more serious was the decision taken in 1926 to move a good 138 Farnese paintings from the Neapolitan gallery to the National Gallery and Town Hall of Parma and to the Palazzo Ducale of Piacenza, in order to set up a civic museum. This was almost, it might be said, in compensation for the presumed 'usurpation' the two Emilian towns had suffered when Charles of Bourbon, in the 18th century, had quite legitimately decided to transfer the family collection to the capital of his Southern Kingdom. This loss was only partly compensated by the introduction into the Gallery of the National Museum of the paintings left in bequest by d'Avalos in 1862 which became part of the Museum collection only in 1882, but even then not all

mounted. It was further compensated by the purchase, between the 19th and 20th centuries, of important works such as the *Crocifissione* (Crucifixion) by Masaccio and the *Ritratto di Luca Pacioli* (Portrait of Luca Pacioli) attributed to Jacopo de' Barbari, and by the transfer of some 'masterpieces' withdrawn from churches in Naples (the panel with *San Ludovico da Tolosa* by Simone Martini for Santa Chiara, and the great 'retable' by Colantonio, both transferred from the church of San Lorenzo Maggiore).

The choice of the new seat for the Gallery was made by a ministerial decree of the 16th May 1949. It fell on the Palace of Capodimonte with a plan drawn up by the architect Ezio de Felice, under the direction of the Superintendent Bruno Molajoli, and financed by the Cassa per il Mezzogiorno. The rooms on the second floor, once used for the staff quarters, had to be completely restored in order to be adapted as exhibition halls. The plan foresaw the following: the extension of the 19th century staircase which earlier had stopped at the first floor; the demolishing of the existing partitions, thus creating large exhibition rooms; the lowering of the ceiling of one of the two great halls on the piano nobile to the level of the other rooms; the substitution of the roofs and of the antique wooden trusses with more modern covering, with roof tiles supported by precompressed aluminium structures and spaced out with tempered plate glass panes to illuminate the underlying rooms; the creation of new ceilings in brickwork with velaria to allow natural light to pass from the attic; the construction of a new engineering plant network placed in the available spaces in the attics. The work began in June 1952 and was completed in five years. It was extended to the piano nobile, in order to improve the presentation of the collection of decorative arts and furnishings which had been there for about a century. For this occasion it was integrated with numerous other items of various origin (from the Royal Palaces of Naples, Portici and Caserta, from Villa Favorita at Herculaneum or from Neapolitan churches long closed to the congregation). In the meantime other changes were taking place. All the paintings, drawings and other items of Medieval and Modern art, then exhibited in the Palazzo degli Studi, were transferred to the new seat of

Capodimonte. (The Palazzo degli Studi was, by that time, reserved exclusively for the presentation of the collections of antiques with the new name of the National Archaeological Museum). The 18th century frescos by Fedele Fischetti, moved from Palazzo Casacalenda and donated by the heirs of Balzo di Presenzano, had been arranged in the vaults of three rooms on the piano nobile. The ceiling in coloured plaster, once in the Royal Palace in Portici, had been again united to the porcelain wall decoration of Maria Amalia's boudoir, and transferred to Capodimonte in 1886. The History of Art Library of the Superintendence, containing more than 20,000 volumes, was now arranged on the first floor and open to the public for consultation. Thus, enriched by a series of integrated technical structures and services essential to the life of a museum (storehouses, workshops, archives, photographic laboratories, carpenter's shop and even a small guest house for foreign and Italian guests), the new museum structure, called the National Gallery and Museum of Capodimonte, was solemnly opened to the public in 1957.

Thanks to all these changes, the Museum was able to respond to new needs. However, it was still detached from the social and cultural reality of a rapidly developing and chaotic city, also because of its distance from the city centre. The selection of antique paintings, destined for the New Gallery on the second floor, was made with scientific severity, and philological and pedagogic accuracy by Ferdinando Bologna, after careful research and restoration. The result of this selection was a succession of panels and canvases which documented many aspects and moments of the history of painting in Italy and other European centres (Flanders in particular, because of the number of Flemish paintings in the Farnese collection) following the traditional criteria of exhibiting by period and school of art. Examples are, among others, *Deposizione* (Entombment) by Polidoro da Caravaggio, *Cristo alla colonna* (Christ at the Pillar) by Battistello Caracciolo, *Elemosina di Santa Lucia* (Charity of Santa Lucia) by Aniello Falcone, the two "still lifes" by Giuseppe and Giovan Battista Recco, *David* by Giovan Battista Spinelli, *Enea e Didone* (Aeneas and Dido) and *Ritratto del principe Tarsia Spinelli in abiti di Cavaliere di San Gennaro* (Portrait of the Prince of Tarsia Spinelli dressed as a knight of Saint Gennaro) by Francesco Solimena, *Ritratto di canonico* (Portrait of a canon) by Gaspare Traversi and *Enea con la Sibilla* (Aeneas with the Sibyl) by Pietro Bardellino, all bought by the state in different years, and the 15th century polyptych with *San Severino*, moved from the church of Santi Severino e Sossio, the big "retable" of Pietro Befulco from the Congregation of the Discipline of the Cross, the *Assunta* (Assumption) by Titian and the *Flagellazione* (Flagellation) by Caravaggio from San Domenico Maggiore, the *Trinitas terrestris* by Jusepe de Ribeira from the Royal Palace, that was once in the Trinità delle Monache, and the *Madonna del Rosario* (Madonna of the Rosary) by Giovanni Lanranco - recovered from the Parish Church of Afragola but once in Monteoliveto and earlier assigned to the Certosa di San Martino. However, although the criteria of presentation adopted by the new National Picture Gallery confirmed the museum choices made in the early 19th century, the new museum adopted new techniques such as the 'mixed lighting' on the second floor. These techniques were later adopted by other museums, both foreign and Italian, when modernising their own structures.

The choices, made on the piano nobile, regarding the new exhibition of the Farnese and Bourbon Armoury, the porcelain collections and the 19th century picture gallery (today numbering little over 900 listed items) were equally good examples. In 1958 Mario De Ciccio donated 1,300 items to be exhibited in a particular section dedicated to the donor. Then, in 1960, more than 100 works of the last century (paintings, drawings and sculptures) coming from the collection of the Banco di Napoli, were added. In 1962 Gustavo Toma bequeathed to the museum 13 paintings by his father Gioacchino; and, remaining in the sphere of Neapolitan paintings of the 19th century, the museum was enriched by the donations of Marino (1957), Marsiconovo and Cenzato (1964), Astarita (1970: 428 paintings, drawings and watercolours by Giacinto Gigante and by the School of Posillipo) and Morisani (1977). Moreover, with regard to the section of the 'minor arts' (which already included more than 17,000 listed items), a remarkable example of a Neapolitan crib of the 18th century, the only item of this type of workmanship present in the collection of

Capodimonte, was added, thanks to the Catello donation in 1986. With regard to the section of 'antique paintings' (today a little more than the 1,950 listed items) exhibited in the new rooms on the second floor of the Museum, we must remember that since 1960 (thanks to generous legacies or donations) some remarkable paintings were added: *il Cavallino* (The Colt) by Pallavicini d'Albaneta; some 'still lifes' by Giuseppe Cenzato (1964); *Andrea de Lione and Paolo de Matteis* by Santangelo Sica (1967); the *Cesare Fracanzano* by Lomonaco Castriota Scandenberg (1971); *il Cavallino* (The Colt) by Giuseppe Marzano (1975). Not a great deal, one might think, compared to other Italian and foreign museums, recipients of more generous public and private donations. But, it is not improbable that similar donations may have been hindered both by the well known deficiencies of Italian legislation and by the difficult social, cultural and economic reality of a city that has always considered Capodimonte as an institution with no real connection with the complex, tormented reality of every day life.

However, at least on its re-opening in 1957, the Museum was considered by many people not only as a new museum but, above all, a museum which was 'new'. This thanks to the facilities created inside, such as a library, a photographic library, a workshop, a café and a stall for the sale of catalogues, postcards and photos. There was also an auditorium with 300 seats, situated in the former Royal Chapel and equipped for lectures, concerts, theatre-shows and film projections. The museum, at that time, had a small selected number of daily visitors and was an oasis of peace and culture far from the madding crowd.

At the end of the seventies all over Naples, at every social level, a new interest in historical happenings and different aspects of the history of arts, was born. In this period the halls were, on many occasions, employed as show places for temporary art exhibitions on different moments and themes in the history of the Arts in Naples. In 1979, after an exhibition of strictly scientific nature on the Naturalist painter Carlo Sellitto (1977), an exhibition on 18th century civilisation was organised, with results beyond all expectations. Unfortunately, the exhibition had to be closed at the end of 1980 for the necessary work of restoration to the Palace, damaged in

the terrible earthquake of 23rd November, when it had already touched a peak of slightly less than 800,000 visitors. This exhibition was followed by many others. The one on "Leonardo e i Leonardeschi" in 1983, and, between 1984 and 1986, the three exhibitions on the "17th century civilisation", "Caravaggio and his times" and on the "French Impressionists from American Museums" which sometimes even touched peaks of 2,000-2,500 visitors per day. A great step ahead, if these figures are compared with those of the 70-80 visitors per day averaged up to then. However, as a consequence, the structural organisation of Capodimonte became inadequate to the necessities imposed by the ever increasing number of culturally diverse visitors. Whereas the museum had been conceived mainly for an *élite* of scholars and Art 'lovers', all this showed how public interests were changing .

Therefore it was necessary to provide for the modernisation of the museum, and to adapt it to the new safety regulations for public buildings. The aim was that of rendering the way of viewing the Museum - its history, origins and its rich art collections - more attractive to a general public, through the creation of new additional services and a change in the traditional order of the exhibition rooms. The Restoration factories and the offices of Superintendence have been moved to the nearby Bourbon building, near the entrance to the park, called the "Great Gate", while the History of Art library has been transferred to Castel Sant'Elmo. Therefore, new exhibition spaces for the permanent collections of art, or for temporary exhibitions have been created. The projects, financed by ministerial funds granted under FIO 1985 and FIO 1986, have been almost completed although with some delays.

Ordinary ministerial funds, earmarked under the laws 64/86 and 449/87 for extraordinary projects, have been used for the works directed towards the recovery and restructuring of the rooms in the Palace on the ground floor and the mezzanine. Here are now a series of conservation rooms, study halls, and temporary exhibitions of artistic material from the new Graphic Department (more than 2,000 drawings and water-colours from the 16th to the 19th centuries and more than 20,000 prints).

14   The new plans have brought considerable changes to the exhibition criteria adopted in 1957 and still valid until the middle eighties when the whole Farnese collection was arranged in the very rooms of the piano nobile previously occupied with the 19th century collection, then temporarily put in storage. In the entrance hall there are the enormous neo-classical canvases of Camuccini, Benvenuti and Hayez, a selection of the most significant Farnese works. On the piano nobile the collection is arranged in chronological order, subdivided in schools and integrated with paintings purchased by the Italian State after 1860 such as the *Crocifissione* (Crucifixion) by Masaccio, for example or the *Ritratto di Luca Pacioli* (Portrait of Luca Pacioli) by Jacopo dei Barbari. However, they bear no relation to the history of painting in Naples after the 13th century. In the adjoining rooms, occupied in the 18th century by the library and the other collections of Casa Farnese transferred to Capodimonte, a new arrangement of the Farnese collection of bronzes, other pieces of jewellery, furniture, and ornaments, has been made. The collection De Ciccio has been kept in the same rooms chosen by Bruno Molajoli in 1958. In some rooms on the piano nobile, once reserved for the modern library of the institute, a collection of paintings, and medieval and modern objects from the collection of Stefano Borgia acquired in 1817, has been arranged. The section of antiquities has obviously stayed at the Archaeological Museum. The historical and chronological order now followed, had not been respected in the arrangement of 1957, which started with objects of the Napoleonic period. The *boudoir* in porcelain, brought from the Royal Palace of Portici, has found its old position in the halls of the Royal Apartment.

The exhibition rooms on the second floor host paintings of various origins, chiefly from the ancient collection created by the monastic suppression of the last century, or recovered from local churches closed to the congregation or damaged by the earthquake of the 23rd November 1980. These paintings witness the history of painting in Naples, from the Byzantine phase of the early 13th century to the 'Realism' of the late 19th century. There are plans, however, to create in the Royal Palace in the city centre, a museum of painting and arts from the 13th to the 19th century.

Again on the second floor, a section has been organised containing works by Andy Warhol and Alberto Burri, who in 1978 donated to Capodimonte his *Grande cretto nero* (Great black crevice). Lucio Amelio in 1994 donated from his collection one of the versions of *Vesuvius* painted by Andy Warhol for the exhibition held in the museum in 1985. Still on the second floor, there are works by other Neapolitan, Italian and foreign artists (Barisani, Spinosa, Alfano, Pisani, Pistoletto, Kounellis, Merz, Mattiacci, Buren, etc.). Finally, as in many other European and American museums, there is also a section which documents aspects or moments in the activity of those many people who, beginning from the end of the first World War and especially in the last few years, have contributed in various ways to the success of Naples and of Capodimonte in the difficult world of contemporary art.

Nicola Spinosa
Superintendent for the Historical
and Artistic Properties of Naples and its province

Antonio Joli, King Ferdinand IV
of Bourbon and his court outside
the Royal Palace of Capodimonte.
Naples, Museo di San Martino

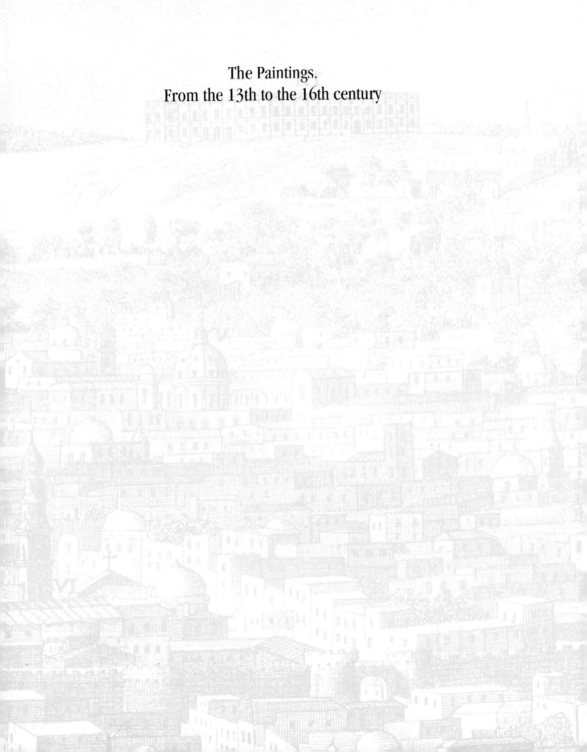

The Paintings.
From the 13th to the 16th century

The Farnese collections, both in Rome and Parma, were almost completely lacking in the so called 'primitive' paintings, therefore the works of Masolino, Mantegna, Bellini and Botticelli were a notable exception. This is why in the picture gallery of Capodimonte, the section of 13th and 14th century painting, and partly also of the 15th century, includes 19th and 20th century purchases or even more recent insertions from churches and convents of the city and the region.

For example, the 13th century is represented by some works on panel of local Byzantine tradition – such as *Santa Maria de Flumine*, coming from the Amalfi coast, whereas the 14th century includes both the great *San Ludovico di Tolosa* painted by Simone Martini in 1317 for the Angevine court of Naples, coming from San Lorenzo, and other notable examples of the Giottesque and Senese presence in town (Roberto d'Oderisio, Niccolò di Tommaso, Lippo and Andrea Vanni). There is also a series of Tuscan small works mainly acquired in 1817 with the Borgia collection of Velletri. Among these stand out the important triptych by Taddeo Gaddi (1336) and the panels by Bernardo Daddi, Jacopo del Casentino, Lippo Vanni and Gualtieri di Giovanni. As for the 15th century, a consistent and convincing image of the Renaissance painting in Florence and in the centre of Italy is reached through several paintings that fit in well with the existing works. They are firstly, the recent acquisition of the formidable cymatium (top moulding of a classical cornice) by Masaccio with the *Crocifissione* (Crucifixion) secondly, all the paintings derived from the Bourbon requisitions in Rome, in 1799 such as the suggestive *Annunciazione* (Annunciation) by Filippino Lippi and the fragments of the juvenile altar-piece painted by Raffaello for Città di Castello. Lastly, the final arrival, from the Neapolitan churches of Monteoliveto and of Santa Caterina at Formiello, of the Assumption by Pinturicchio and the *Strage degli Innocenti* (Slaughter of the Innocent) by Matteo di Giovanni, the two Masolino from Santa Maria Maggiore, the juvenile *Madonna* by Botticelli and other panels – Farnese and not – by Mainardi and Caporali, by Signorelli and Perugino, by Lorenzo di Credi and Raffaellino del Garbo. The same can be said of the Venetian area. Few works but each of great quality outline the acquisition of a new sense of colour, light and nature around the 15th and 16th

century: *Sant'Eufemia* Borgia by Mantegna, the *Ritratto di Luca Pacioli* (Portrait of Luca Pacioli) by the presumed Jacopo dei Barbari and other paintings by Bartolomeo or Alvise Vivarini, up to Palma the Elder. They were all introduced to the collection in the 19th century and are in harmony with the Farnese paintings, the *Ritrattino Gonzaga* (Small Portrait of Gonzaga) by Mantegna, the *Trasfigurazione* (Transfiguration) by Bellini and the juvenile paintings by Lotto.

Very different and much richer is the situation of the museum collections concerning the 16th century. The Farnese collections, brought to Naples by Charles of Bourbon, already numbered many works of the 16th century, chiefly Emilian, but also coming from Tusco-roman, Venetian and Flemish areas. Therefore, the Bourbon and post-Unitarian acquisitions simply filled some gaps in the collection itself or further strengthened an already enviable selection - as in the case of the work by Titian from San Domenico Maggiore.

The group of Tuscan authors included from the beginning Farnese works such as the *Sacrificio* (Sacrifice) by Pontormo, the *Ritratti* (Portraits) by Rosso, Salviati, Maso di San Friano and other panels by Vasari, Puligo and Brescianino. This group was also integrated - at the beginning of the 19th century - with the altar-pieces by Fra Bartolomeo and by Sodoma. Both are examples of the classicistic tendency in fashion between Florence and Siena at the beginning of the century. The altar-piece by Fra Bartolomeo had been requisitioned in Rome from the French, who, in their turn, had stolen it in Prato. The altar-piece by Sodoma had been taken from the Neapolitan church of San Tommaso. The collection has always been equally rich in works of the artists active in Rome. Many of these works had been commissioned or collected by the Farnese throughout the centuries. The most notable are the portraits of *Cardinale Alessandro* and of Pope *Leone X con due cardinali* (Leone X with two Cardinals), the *Madonne 'del Divino Amore'* (Madonnas 'of the Divine Love'), of *del velo* (The Veil), and *del passeggio* by Raffaello and his workshop, and also the famous *Madonna della gatta* by Giulio Romano, the three important works by Sebastiano del Piombo and the copy of the Sistine *Giudizio* (Judgement) by Michelangelo, completed by Venusti for Cardinal Alessandro. This group was integrated – between the end of the 18th century and today – with some paintings by the other apprentice of Raffaello and champion of the 'Manner style', Polidoro da Caravaggio. These paintings were already in Naples but housed in a different location or coming from Messina.

Most of the works of the Venetians are made up of the famous group by Titian, commissioned by the Farnese family since 1543 and realised mainly in Rome in 1545-46. This group consists of the many portraits of *Paolo III* and of the other members of the Farnese family, and the *Danae*. They form a unique, compact example in the research of the artist, by then mature, on the use of light. In the last century to these paintings were added the two rare canvases painted in Rome by the young El Greco, the grand painting by Pordenone coming from Corte-maggiore (both 'Farnese'), and other works by Schiavone, Tintoretto and Bassano, in a kind of swift survey of the Venetian culture between the colouristic tradition and the influences of 'Mannerism'. The works of the northern painters also have Farnese origin. They are the extraordinary couple – *Ciechi* (the Blind) and *Misantropo* (the Misanthrope) – by Bruegel, the series of *Mercati* (Markets) by Beuckelaer and de Muyser and the other notable paintings by Wit, de Vos, de Witte, Bles and Sons. These works are all Farnese and most of them came directly from Flanders at the time when Alessandro governed there. Sometimes they arrived thanks to nobles of the Parmesan court which followed Alessandro, such as the Masi. Exceptions to this group are perhaps the *Adultera* (Adulteress) by Cranach and the two beautiful triptychs by Joos van Cleve, included in the Bourbon collection between the 18th and 19th century.

Anyhow, because of the Farnese roots of the museum, the Emilian and Padan schools are represented better than any other school. First of all the Parmisans, with many masterpieces by Correggio, - *Zingarella* (the Gypsy girl), *Nozze di Santa Caterina* (the Nuptials of Saint Catherine), and *San Giuseppe col donatore* (Saint Joseph with donor). The following works, which used to be in the Neapolitan picture gallery of the Girolamini, were added at the beginning of the century: the *Sant'Antonio, Antea, Lucrezia, Sacra Famiglia* (Holy Family), *Galeazzo San Vitale*, all by Parmigianino besides some masterpieces by Anselmi, Orsi, Mazzola Bedoli. Through this group of works it is possible to fully

follow the development of a local school from the serene classicism of its beginning to the highly sophisticated and intellectual 'Manner' style. The Ferraresi are present with the small Farnese paintings by Dosso Dossi and Garofalo, to which the great *Pietà* by Ortolano and a series of works by Scarsellino were conveniently added, thanks to the 19th century requisitions from San Luigi dei Francesi in Rome and from Montecassino and, later, to the d'Avalos donation (1862). The Lumbard painters include followers of Leonardo's style but also Luini, Moretto, Cesare da Sesto, Boccaccino Campi. Finally, the Bolognese, are represented in the collection first with the 'mannerists' – Tibaldi, Sammacchini, Calvaert – and then chiefly with the Academy of the Carracci, of which it is possible to follow the whole evolution, from the Po school to the old fashioned classicism of Annibale, with a series of works which have no equals perhaps in any other museum in the world: from *Rinaldo e Armida* by Ludovico to the one by Annibale, from the juvenile *Ritratti di musici* (Portrait of musicians) by Agostino and Annibale to the *Democrito* (Democritus) by the said Agostino, from the *Nozze di Santa Caterina* (Nuptials of Saint Catherine) by the young Annibale, in the style of Correggio, to the masterpieces of his later years – the *Fiume* (River), *Bacco* (Bacchus), *Ercole al bivio* (Hercules at the cross-roads), and the *Pietà*.

The Neapolitan 15th-16th century paintings chiefly came from the churches of the town, at the period of the suppression of the monastic Orders or also, more recently, so that they could be safely stored. Among them, the paintings by Colantonio, once part of the 'retable' of San Lorenzo stand out. They are almost a symbol of the Hispano-Flemish and Mediterranean nature of the southern Renaissance. The mysterious 'Strozzi panel' – purchased in 1904 – illustrates the image of the city on the sea at the time of the Aragonese sovereigns. As for the still little known Neapolitan artists of the 16th century, the museum counts a vast sampling of them, from the Raffaelism of the beginning of the century, typical of Andrea da Salerno, to the 'mannerism' of the Tuscan immigrant Marco Pino and the Counter-reformation atmosphere of the various Curia, Hendricksz and Santafede, precursors of the revolutionary arrival in Naples of Michelangelo da Caravaggio.

Unknown master from Campania
13th century
Santa Maria de Flumine
1290 ca.
tempera on panel; cm 200x88
source: Amalfi, Santa Maria de Flumine,
in storage
inventory: Q 1090

Simone Martini
San Ludovico di Tolosa
1317
signed on the predella «Symon de Senis
me pinxit»
tempera on panel; central panel
cm 200x138, predella cm 56x138
source: Naples, San Lorenzo Maggiore
(first inclusion 1927)
inventory: Q. 34
It is one of the masterpieces of Simone
Martini and of Italian Gothic painting,
done probably in 1317 for the cano-
nisation of Ludovico, elder brother of
Robert of Anjou, king of Naples, to
whom he had left the throne. The
sumptuous aspect of the two portraits,
the magnificence of the materials and
the corrective interpretation with which
the stories of the Franciscan saint and
the pauper are shown in the predella,
are part of a complex political project
aimed at the exaltation of the image of
the 'royal' holiness of the family.

22

Taddeo Gaddi
Trittico con Madonna e Santi
(Triptych with the Holy Virgin
and Saints)
1336
Tempera on panel; cm 66x57
source: Velletri, Borgia Museum
(purchased 1817)
inventory: S 84303

Roberto di Oderisio
Crocifissione
(Crucifixion)
1335 ca.
Tempera on panel; cm 130x189
source: Naples Museum of San Martino,
in storage

Masolino da Panicale
Assunzione della Vergine
(Assumption of the Holy Virgin)
1428 ca.
tempera on panel; cm 142x76
source: Farnese collection
inventory: Q 33

24

Masolino da Panicale
Fondazione di Santa Maria Maggiore
(Foundation of Santa Maria Maggiore)
1428
Tempera on panel; cm 143x76
source: Farnese collection
inventory: Q 42
Together with the *Assunta* (Assumption)
this was the centre of a triptych painted
on both sides by Masolino and Masaccio
in 1428 for the Church of Santa Maria
Maggiore in Rome. Pope Liberio is

represented here while founding the
Basilica just where a miraculous snowfall
has taken place.

Masaccio
Crocifissione
(Crucifixion)
1426
Tempera on panel; cm 83x63.5
source: Naples, De Simone collection
(purchased 1901)
inventory: Q 36

Bought in 1901 for the museum, it was
the top part of the polyptych painted by
Masaccio in 1426 for the church of the
Carmine in Pisa, now divided among
the museums of London, Berlin, Pisa
and Malibu. The great artist, father of
the Tuscan Renaissance, fully expresses
in it his revolutionary feeling of space
and colour, together with the study of
the human body.

Sandro Botticelli
Madonna con Bambino e Angeli
(Holy Virgin with Child and Angels)
1455-1460 ca.
tempera on panel; cm 100x71
source: Farnese collection
inventory: Q 46

It is among the masterpieces of Botticelli's youth, during the time - around 1470 - in which he was still developing his art under the influence of Filippo Lippi and the Verrocchio. In the Farnese Palace, where it comes from, it was attributed to Filippo Lippi.

Filippino Lippi
Annunciazione e Santi
(Annunciation and Saints)
1490 ca.
tempera on panel; cm 114x124
source: Rome, storage San Luigi dei
Francesi (requisition 1800)
inventory: Q 42
It arrived in Naples, at the Gallery of
Francavilla, in 1801, coming from the
store room arranged by the French
republican troops in Rome, where it was
attributed to the Ghirlandaio. Berenson
identified it as a juvenile work by
Filippino Lippi, around 1485. It shows a
beautiful view of Florence in the centre
background, with the Bargello, the
Badia and Santa Maria del Fiore.

Raffaellino del Garbo
Madonna con Bambino
e San Giovannino
(Madonna with Child and
Saint Giovannino)
tempera on panel; diameter cm 85.5
source: Naples, Carafa d'Andria
collection (purchased 1834)
inventory: Q 43

30

Pinturicchio
Assunzione della Vergine
(Assumption of the Virgin)
1510 ca.
tempera on panel; cm 278x173
source: Naples, Monteoliveto
(first inclusion from the suppressed
monasteries 1802)
inventory: Q 49

Matteo di Giovanni
Strage degli Innocenti
(The slaughter of the Innocent)
1480-90 ca.
tempera on panel; cm 237x238
source: Naples, Santa Caterina
a Formiello
(first inclusion from the suppressed
monasteries 1806)
inventory: Q 38

Andrea Mantegna
Sant'Eufemia
1454
tempera on canvas; cm 190x95
source: Velletri, Borgia Museum
(purchased 1817)
inventory: Q 61

33

Andrea Mantegna
Ritratto del Cardinale Gonzaga
(Portrait of Cardinal Gonzaga)
1460 ca.
oil on panel; cm 73.9x66
source: Farnese collection
inventory: Q 60
It comes from the collection of Fulvio
Orsini and was then moved to Palazzo
Farnese in Rome where it was believed
to be the work of Giovanni Bellini. In
1895 it was recognised as the work of
Mantegna. The character represented
might be Francesco Gonzaga, already
elected Cardinal at the age of sixteen, in
1461, and later represented by the artist
in the frescos of the Nuptial Chamber at
Mantua.

Giovanni Bellini
Trasfigurazione
(The Transfiguration)
1480-85 ca.
oil on panel, cm 115x154
signed lower centre
«IONNES BELLI»
source: the Farnese collection
inventory: Q 56

Already in the 17th century it was one of the most important works of the collection of Palazzo Farnese in Rome, perhaps coming from the Fioccardo chapel of the Cathedral of Vicenza. Signed at the bottom, it is datable at about 1480-85. Typical of this period of Giovanni Bellini are the new and deep feeling for nature, colour and light.

Alvise Vivarini
Trittico. Madonna con Bambino tra i
Santi Francesco e Bernardino
(Triptych. Madonna with Child between
the Saints Francis and Bernardino)
1485
tempera on panel: central panel
cm 120x50, side panels cm 116x39
source: Naples, Giacomo Filioli
collection (purchased 1831)
inventory: Q 53

Jaco. Bar
Ritratto di Fra Luca Pacioli
(Portrait of Fra Luca Pacioli)
1495
oil on panel; cm 99x120
signed and dated lower left
«IACO. BAR. VIGEN/NIS. 1495»
source: Naples, Eustachio Rogadeo di
Torrequadra collection (purchased
1903)
inventory: Q 58

The great mathematician and expert in
perspective is portrayed at a table with
two books, the *Elements* by Euclid and
the *Summa* by Pacioli himself. The
painting was both in Urbino and in
Florence. Its author is uncertain but the
Venetian inspiration is clear and since
Piero della Francesca's times the critics
have often doubted the attribution of the
work to the Venetian Jacopo de' Barbari,
suggested by the scroll down on the right.

Colantonio
San Francesco consegna la Regola
(Saint Francis hands over the Rule)
1445 ca.
oil on panel; cm 174x149
source: Naples, San Lorenzo Maggiore
(first inclusion from the suppressed
monasteries 1808) inventory: Q 21
Together with the *San Gerolamo nello
studio* (Saint Jerome in the study) now
also in Capodimonte, it was part of a two
storey altar-piece painted by Colantonio

around 1445 for the Franciscan basilica
of San Lorenzo in Naples. It was once
sided by small columns with figures of
Santi (Saints) and *Beati* (Blessed souls)
of the order, now scattered in various
private collections. The Neapolitan artist,
master of Antonello da Messina, shows
his debt to the Mediterranean culture of
realistic tradition and his Flemish origin,
along with artists such as the provençal
Barthelemy d'Eyck or the Valentian
Jacomart Baço.

38

Colantonio
San Gerolamo nello studio
(St. Jerome in the study)
1445 ca.
oil on panel: cm 125x151
source: Naples, San Lorenzo Maggiore
(first inclusion from the suppressed
monasteries 1808)
inventory: Q 20

Unknown, end 15th century
(attr. to F. Pagano or F. Rosselli)
Veduta di Napoli col ritorno della flotta aragonese
(View of Naples on the return of the Aragonese fleet)

tempera on panel; cm 245x82
source: Florence, Palazzo Strozzi
(purchased 1910)
Naples, Museum of San Martino,
in storage

Pedro Fernández
Polittico della Visitazione
(Polyptych of the Visitation)
1510 ca.
oil on panel;
Adorazione dei Magi
(Adoration of the Magi)
inventory: Q 801, cm 127.5x62.8

Visitazione (Visitation)
inventory: Q 801, cm 127x118.3
Natività (Nativity)
inventory: Q 801, cm 127.5x62.8
source: Naples, Santa Maria delle Grazie
a Caponapoli
(first inclusion from the suppressed
monasteries ante 1821)

42

**Raffaello and Evangelista
di Pian di Meleto**
Cristo e la Vergine
(Christ and the Virgin) 1501
tempera on panel; cm 111x74
source: Rome, storage San Luigi dei
Francesi; from Città di Castello,
Sant'Agostino (requisition 1800)
inventory: Q 50

Raffaello (attr.)
Ritratto del Cardinale Alessandro Farnese
(Portrait of Cardinal Alessandro Farnese)
first quarter of the 16th century
oil on panel; cm 138x91
source: Farnese collection
inventory: Q 145

from Raffaello
Ritratto di Leone X con due cardinali
(Portrait of Leone X with two Cardinals)
first quarter of the 16th century
oil on panel, cm 152x112
source: Farnese collection
inventory: Q 138

Workshop of Raffaello
Madonna del passeggio
(the Madonna walking)
first quarter of the 16th century
oil on panel; cm 87x62
source: Farnese collection
inventory: Q 148

Workshop of Raffaello
(Giovan Francesco Penni)
Madonna del Divino Amore
(Madonna of the Divine Love)
1520 ca.
oil on panel; cm 137x111
source: Farnese collection
inventory: Q 146

Giulio Romano
Madonna della gatta
(Madonna with cat)
1523 ca.
oil on panel; cm 172x144
source: Farnese collection
inventory: Q 140

48

Sebastiano del Piombo
Sacra Famiglia
(Holy Family)
1530 ca.
oil laid on board; cm 113x88
source: Farnese collection
inventory: Q 149

Sebastiano del Piombo
Ritratto di Clemente VII
(Portrait of Clement VII)
1526 ca.
oil on canvas; cm 147x100
source: Farnese collection
inventory: Q 147
It was in the collection of Fulvio Orsini, librarian and counsellor of the Cardinals Alessandro and Odoardo Farnese, from which it passed as a gift (1600) to the Roman palace of the family. The Pope is portrayed without a beard, that is before the Sack of Rome in 1527 and the artist creates one of his best portraits. Under Michelangelo's influence the colour, of Venetian origin, though with icy tones, is compressed in a powerful outlined mass.

Marcello Venusti
Copia del 'Giudizio Universale'
di Michelangelo
(Copy of the «Last Judgement»
by Michelangelo)
1550 ca.
oil on panel; cm 190x145
source: Farnese Collection
inventory: Q. 139
This is the copy of the *Giudizio* (Last
Judgement) painted by Michelangelo in
the Sistine Chapel in the Vatican
uncovered in 1541. The work was
commissioned to Venusti by Cardinal
Alessandro Farnese in 1549. Venusti's
copy was painted before the Council of
Trent in 1564, that is, when the original
still displayed nude figures, and before
its subsequent restoration. This is why it
represents a very important document
for the understanding of Michelangelo's
original work.

51

Polidoro da Caravaggio
Trasporto di Cristo al sepolcro
(Transport of Christ to the Sepulchre)
1527 ca.
oil on panel; cm 106x81
source: Naples, Irene Montemayor
Collection (purchased 1971)
inventory: Q 1774

52

Polidoro da Caravaggio
Andata al Calvario
(The ascent of Calvary)
1530-1534
oil on panel; cm 130x247
source: Messina, Annunziata detta dei
Catalani (first inclusion before 1799)
inventory: Q 103

Pontormo
Scena di sacrificio
(Scene of sacrifice)
1520 ca.
tempera on canvas; cm 85x148
source: Farnese Collection
inventory: Q 1039
It is an important but little known work
by the great Florentine artist
representative of Mannerism, probably
painted in the early twenties, when
Pontormo was under the strong
influence of the study of the northern
prints. Attributed to Raffaello in the
Farnese collections, the «grisaille»
(technique of monochrome painting)
represents a mysterious scene of sacrifice
or worship.

54

Fra' Bartolomeo
Assunta
(The Assumption) 1518
oil on panel; cm 330x202
source: Rome, stored in San Luigi dei
Francesi from Prato, Santa Maria in
Castello (Requisition 1800)
inventory: Q 100

Rosso Fiorentino
Ritratto di giovane
(Portrait of a young man)
1527 ca.
oil on panel, cm 120x86
source: Farnese collection
inventory: Q 112
It is the portrait of a young man inside a room. We can catch a glimpse of the door framed by telamones (columns in the form of a male figure) and of the unmade beds, a painting, a tapestry and the table, covered by an Anatolian carpet, on which the young man himself is sitting. This very "setting", the links with Parmigianino - to whom in fact in the past the portrait had been attributed in the Orsini and Farnese collections - and the fact that the painting has been left unfinished, suggest that perhaps Rosso worked on it in Rome during the Sack (1527).

Francesco Salviati
Ritratto di uomo
(Portrait of a man)
1545-1548 ca.
oil on panel, cm 75.5x58.5
source: Farnese collection
inventory: Q 142

Giorgio Vasari
Resurrezione
(Resurrection) 1545
oil on panel; cm 117x73
source: Naples, Monteoliveto
(first inclusion from the suppressed
monasteries before 1821)
inventory: Q 1052

After Michelangelo
(Hendrik van der Broecke, attr.)
Venere e Amore
(Venus and Cupid)
III quarter of the 16th century
oil on panel; cm 120x195
source: Farnese collection
inventory: Q 748

Peter de Witte
Sacra Famiglia
(The Holy Family)
III quarter of the 16th century
oil on panel; cm 107x86
source: Farnese collection
inventory: Q 137

Ludovico Cardi
(known as 'il Cigoli')
Pietà
1596-1600 ca.
oil on panel; cm 101x76
source: Farnese collection
inventory: Q 738

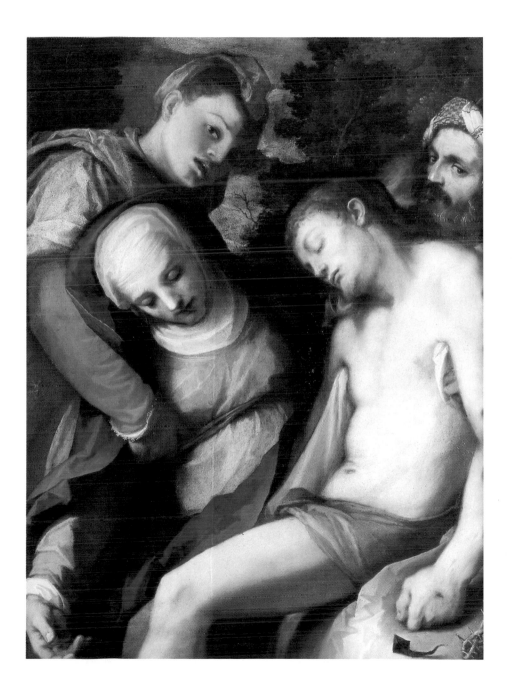

Dosso Dossi
Sacra Conversazione
(Holy Conversation) 1510 ca.
oil on panel; cm 50x73.5
source: Farnese collection
inventory: Q 276
Recognised by Roberto Longhi as the
main work made by the young Dosso,
this painting comes from the collections
of Palazzo Farnese in Rome, where it
had always been attributed to Perugino.
In spite of some conflicting opinions, it
is the most concrete proof - datable
around 1510 - of the importance of
Dosso's journey to Venice and of his first
period of training when he came in
contact with Giorgione, Cariani,
Savoldo and later the young Titian.

**Giovani Battista Benvenuti,
(known as Ortolano)**
Pietà 1520 ca.
oil on panel; cm 273x172
source: Rome, stored in San Luigi dei
Francesi; from Ferrara, San Cristoforo
degli Esposti
(requisition 1800)
inventory: Q 73

Correggio
Sant'Antonio Abate
1515 ca.
oil on panel; cm 48x38
source: Naples, Picture gallery of the
Girolamini (purchased 1906)
inventory: Q 105
This painting was once in the picture
gallery - developed in 16th and 17th
century - of the Oratorian Fathers of
Naples where it was attributed to the
local artist Andra Sabatini. Later, Venturi
attributed the work to Correggio, and
this is the oldest work of the great
Emilian artist present in the museum,
datable at about 1515-16. At this time,
the artist's early training received from
Mantegna, Costa and the Ferraresi at the
beginning of the 16th century, had been
enriched by his following Leonardo's
style.

64

Correggio
Nozze mistiche di Santa Caterina
(Mystic nuptials of Saint Catherine)
1520 ca.
oil on panel; cm 28.5x23.5
source: Farnese collection
inventory: Q 106
It comes from the collection of Barbara
Sanseverino Sanvitale, countess of Sala,
and was acquired by the Farnese in
1612, on the occasion of the
confiscation of the properties of the
rebel feudal lords.
Even then esteemed "a jewel of extreme
beauty", it has been unanimously
considered by the critics as one of the
main examples of the serene classicism
of Correggio, and done around the
period of his supposed journey to Rome
in 1518.

Correggio
San Giuseppe e donatore
(Saint Joseph and donor)
1529
tempera on canvas; cm 167x63
each panel
source: Farnese collection
inventory: Q 1290-1291

Parmigianino
Ritratto di Galeazzo Sanvitale
(Portrait of Galeazzo Sanvitale)
1524
signed and dated on the back «Opus de Mazolla 1524/F.»
oil on panel; cm 109x81
source: Farnese collection
inventory: Q 111
It portrays Galeazzo Sanvitale. In the same years Parmigianino had painted, in a well known small room of his castle, the 'Storie di Diana' (Stories of Diana).
It is the masterpiece done by the young artist before his departure for Rome. The painting became part of the Farnese collection, maybe when Eucherio Sanvitale, Galeazzo's son, sold the family mansion in Parma.

Parmigianino
Sacra Famiglia
(Holy Family)
1527 ca.
tempera on canvas; cm 159x131
source: Farnese collection
inventory: Q 110

Parmigianino
Antea
1530-1535
oil on canvas; cm 135x88
source: Farnese collection
inventory: Q 108
Known as the portrait of Parmigianino's *Innamorata* (Lover), that is of the famous Roman 'cortigiana' (Lady of the court) Antea, it rather represents a young woman in elegant clothes and marten stole. The artist painted it with a keen psychological sense and great attention to the optical properties of the use of mirrors. Painted at the height of Parmigianino's career as an artist (1531-35), on his return to Parma after his stay in Rome and Bologna.

Girolamo Mazzola Bedoli
Sacra Conversazione
(Holy Conversation)
1535 ca.
oil on panel; cm 194x146
source: Farnese collection
inventory: Q 923

Girolamo Mazzola Bedoli
Ritratto di sarto
(Portrait of a tailor)
1540-45 ca.
oil on canvas; cm 88x71
source: Farnese collection
inventory: Q 120

Girolamo Mazzola Bedoli
Annunciazione
(Annunciation)
1550-60 ca.
oil on panel; cm 230x159
source: Farnese collection
inventory: Q 121
It comes from the church of the
Annunziata in Viadana and was sold by

its priests in 1713 to the duke of Parma
Francesco Farnese.
The work was once attributed to
Parmigianino, who probably made the
sketch, now kept at the Metropolitan
Museum of New York. The Annunciation
is, instead, a mature work of his brother-
in-law and follower, Girolamo Mazzola
Bedoli.

Lelio Orsi
San Giorgio e il Drago
(Saint George and the dragon)
1550 ca.
oil on canvas; cm 60x48
source: Farnese collection
inventory: Q 83
It was acquired in 1710 by the Farnese from the merchant Canopi of Bologna as a work by Lelio Orsi. It arrived in Naples in 1734 with Charles of Bourbon and for a long period it was attributed to the Flemish school until 1911 when De Rinaldis recognised it as the work by the artist from Reggio Emilia.
This painting is a later work of Orsi, rich in Roman and 'Correggio' features.

Pellegrino Tibaldi
Sacra Famiglia
(Holy Family)
1550-52 ca.
oil on panel; cm 86x68
source: Farnese collection
inventory: Q 851
It was kept in the Palazzo Farnese in
Rome in the 17th century as an
anonymous work and was attributed to
Tibaldi only in 1956 by Bologna. The
mannerist language which tends to
amplify the shapes in a monumental
manner, is typical of Tibaldi whose
frescos of Palazzo Poggi (1550-52) in
Bologna bear resemblance.

Boccaccio Boccaccino
Adorazione dei Pastori
(Adoration of the shepherds)
1500 ca.
oil on panel; cm 127x100
source: Rome, stored in San Luigi
dei Francesi (requisition 1800)
inventory: Q 68

Bernardino Luini
Madonna con Bambino
(Madonna with Child)
1510-20 ca.
oil on panel; cm 84x65
source: Naples, Durand collection
(purchased 1801)
inventory: Q 92

76

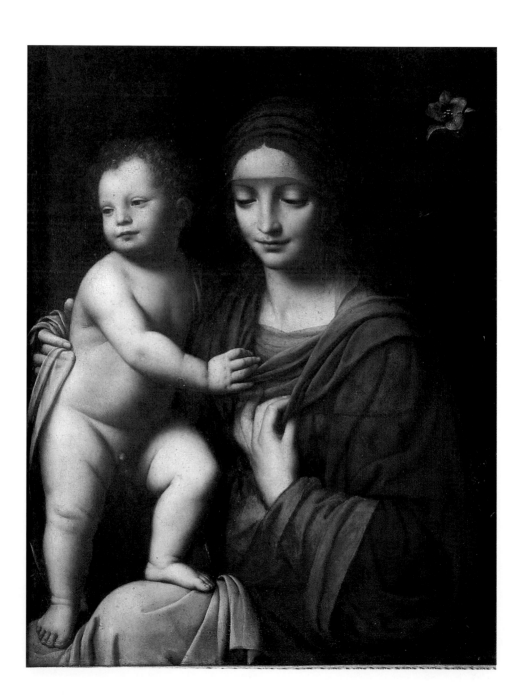

Lorenzo Lotto
Ritratto del vescovo Bernardo de' Rossi
(Portrait of the Bishop Bernardo de' Rossi)
1505
oil on panel; cm 51.5x43.5
source: Farnese collection
inventory: Q 57
This portrait of de' Rossi, Archbishop of Treviso, is perhaps to be identified with the analogous painting mentioned in a Venetian inventory of his properties of 1511. In the 17th century it then passed to the Farnese collections in Parma. It is a juvenile work of Lotto. His «covering» work - an *Allegoria* (Allegory) with the coat of arms of the bishop, now in the Washington Museum - bears the date 1505 and the painter's signature.

Jacopo Palma the Elder
Sacra conversazione con ritratti di donatori
(Holy Conversation with portraits of donors) 1525 ca.
oil on panel; cm 134x200
source: Naples, Barbaja Gallery (purchased 1841)
inventory: Q 84
The Bourbons bought this picture, which is considered one of the most prestigious 19th century additions to the Museum, from the collection of the Neapolitan theatre manager Barbaja. For the serene atmosphere and bright colours of his *Sacre Conversazioni* (Holy Conversations) Palma drew inspiration from the young Titian, obtaining considerable commercial success.

Lorenzo Lotto
Sacra Conversazione
(Holy Conversation)
1503
oil on panel; cm 55.5x86.5
source: Farnese collection
inventory: Q 55

Antonio Solario
Madonna con Bambino e donatore
(Madonna with Child and donor)
1500-10 ca.
oil on panel; cm 85x66
source: London, Langton Douglas
collection
(purchased 1906)
inventory: Q 54

Giovanni Antonio de Sacchis
(known as il Pordenone)
Disputa dell'Immacolata Concezione
(Discussion about the Immaculate
Conception)
1528 ca.
oil on panel; cm 298x198
source: Farnese collection
inventory: Q 86

Titian
Danae, 1545 ca.
oil on canvas; cm 149x202
source: Farnese collection
inventory: Q 134
Derived from the *Metamorphosis* by Ovid, the famous scene of the love story between Danae and Zeus - transformed into golden rain - was painted by Titian in Rome in 1544-46 for the cardinal Alessandro Farnese, who was to keep it in his private rooms. The work represents the highest achievement of Titian's in his late career in terms of light effects. Michelangelo, who saw it while being painted appreciated the colours but found the drawing of poor quality.

Titian
Paolo III con i nipoti
(Paul III with his nephews), 1545 ca.
oil on canvas; cm 202x176
source: Farnese collection
inventory: Q 129
Represents Pope Paul III, at the end of his life, among his nephews Ottavio and Alessandro Farnese, and was probably commissioned to Titian by the latter who - being a cardinal - with this work wanted to ratify his and his brother's role in continuing the family politics. An absolute masterpiece of Titian's later years, it draws inspiration from Raffaello's *Ritratto di Leone X con i cardinali* (Portrait of Leone X with the cardinals).

Titian
Paolo III con camauro
(Paul III with 'camauro' - a type
of cap)
1545 ca.
oil on canvas; cm 126x103
source: Farnese collection
inventory: Q 1135

Titian
Maddalena
(Magdalene)
1550-1560 ca.
oil on canvas; cm 128x103
source: Farnese collection

Titian
Annunciazione
(Annunciation)
1557 ca.
oil on canvas; cm 280x193.5
Signed «Titianus F.»
source: Naples, San Domenico
Maggiore, stored
It comes from the chapel founded by
Cosimo Pinelli in San Domenico
Maggiore in 1557. In the local guide

book of D'Engenio in 1623, it was
already considered as a work by Titian.
For a long time it was believed to be the
copy that Luca Giordano had painted
for a viceroy, as mentioned by De
Dominici (1742/45).
Giordano's copy is, in reality, kept in
Madrid, in the church of San Ginés,
whereas the painting in Naples is now
unanimously considered to be the
original by Titian.

El Greco
Giovinetto che soffia su un carbone
acceso
(Young boy blowing on a burning coal)
1570-1575 ca.
oil on canvas; cm 77.2x68
source: Farnese collection
inventory: Q 192

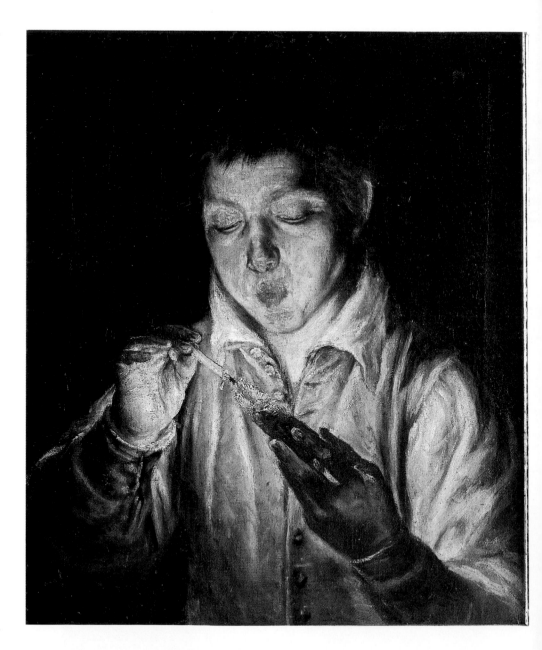

El Greco
Giulio Clovio
1570-1575
oil on canvas; cm 62.5x86.5
source: Farnese collection
inventory: Q 191
This is a portrait of the miniaturist of Croatian origin, Giulio Clovio, for a long time in the service of the Farnese and author, for Cardinal Alessandro, of the famous *Libro d'Ore* (Book of Hours) now on show at the Pierpont Morgan Library of New York.
It is the most significant work of El Greco's Roman period (1570-75), who in it immortalised both his friend and the well known manuscript, probably by request of their mutual host in Palazzo Farnese, the librarian and humanist Fulvio Orsini. The painting, in fact, comes from his collection.

Konrad Witz
Sacra conversazione
(Holy Conversation)
1440-45 ca.
Tempera on panel; 68x41
source: Farnese collection
inventory: Q 4

Joos van Cleve
Adorazione dei Magi
(Adoration of the Magi)
1515 ca.
Triptych oil on panel;
cm 115x93 115x40 115x40
source: Bourbon collection
(purchased 1800)
inventory: Q12

Lucas Cranach the Elder
Cristo e l'adultera
(Christ and the adulteress)
II quarter of 16th century
oil on panel; cm 56x77
source: Bourbon collection
inventory: Q 13

89

Joachim Beuckelaer
Mercato del Pesce
(Fish market)
1570
oil on canvas; cm 155x214
source: Farnese collection
inventory: Q 163

Pieter Bruegel the Elder
Misantropo
(Misanthrope), 1568
tempera on canvas; cm 85x85
source: Farnese collection
inventory: Q 12
The picture represents a misanthrope, shunning the world which is stealing his purse. The work aims at illustrating the Flemish proverb transcribed at the foot «Since the world is so untrustworthy, I go into mourning». It comes from Cosimo Masi's collection, counsellor of Alessandro Farnese in Flanders, during the '80's. After the rebellion of the feudal lords from Parma against the Farnese it was expropriated by Duke Ranuccio I (1612)

Pieter Bruegel the Elder
Parabola dei ciechi
(Parable of the blind)
1568
tempera on canvas; cm 86x154
source: Farnese collection
inventory: Q 1

Jan Sons
Bacco e Arianna
(Bacchus and Ariadne)
1580-90 ca.
oil on canvas, cm 61x39
source: Farnese collection
inventory: Q 1349

94

Jan Sons
Apollo e Dafne
(Apollo and Daphne)
1580-90 ca.
oil on canvas; cm 61x40
source: Farnese collection
inventory: Q 1348

Herri Met de Bles, known as
il Civetta (the Owl)
Il Buon Samaritano
(The good Samaritan)
II quarter of the 16th century
oil on panel 28.5x43
inventory: Q 674

Annibale Carracci
Nozze mistiche di Santa Caterina
(Mystic nuptials of Saint Cathcrine)
1585 ca.
oil on canvas, cm 160x128
source: Farnese collection;
from the store room in the Royal Palace
of Naples
Main work of the young Annibale, it was
painted around 1585 in Parma, under

the strong influence of the art of
Correggio, for the Duke Ranuccio
Farnese. According to Bellori (1672)
and Malvasia (1678) the painter himself
later brought the painting to Rome
(1595) as a gift from Ranuccio to his
brother, the cardinal Odoardo, and as a
'presentation card' of his qualities as
follower of the 16th century classicism
of Correggio and Raffaello.

Annibale Carracci
Ercole al bivio
(Hercules at the cross-roads), 1596
oil on canvas, cm 168x238
source: Farnese collection
inventory: Q 365
It was painted by Annibale in 1596 for
Cardinal Odoardo, as the centre of the
ceiling of a small room of the Farnese
Palace dedicated to Hercules and
painted with other scenes from the myth
of the hero, symbolising the 'virtuous
life'. The canvas, based on classical
models like the Ares Ludovisi, illustrates
in particular the allegorical tale of
Prodico of Ceo referred to by Senofonte.
Hercules, is uncertain between
«Voluptuousness that indicates to him
the easy way» of earthly pleasure, and
Virtue «that indicates to him the steep
and tiring ascent.... that leads to
heaven» (Bellori 1672)

Annibale Carracci
Allegoria fluviale
(River allegory)
1590-95
oil on canvas; cm 108x94
source: Farnese collection
inventory: Q 132

Annibale Carracci
Pietà, 1600 ca.
oil on canvas, cm 158x152
source: Farnese collection
inventory: Q 363
Bellori states that Annibale probably
painted this subject of devotion for
Cardinal Odoardo Farnese in Rome.
It has always been one of the most
representative paintings of the collection
and is one of the best results of the
monumental classicism of the artist,
inspired by the ideal model of the *Pietà*
by Michelangelo.

Ludovico Carracci
Rinaldo e Armida
1583
oil on canvas; cm 166x237
source: Farnese collection
inventory: Q 360
The subject is taken from *Orlando*
Furioso by Ludovico Ariosto

Agostino Carracci
*Arrigo Peloso, Amon nano
e Pietro Matto*
1598 ca.
oil on canvas; cm 97x130
source: Farnese collection
inventory: Q 369
The three characters here represented
were court jesters of Cardinal Odoardo
Farnese in Rome.

102

The Paintings.
The 17th and 18th centuries

The integration of the Farnese and Bourbon collections, together with the 19th and early 20th centuries acquisitions, donations and purchases form a significant example of the different pictorial schools which coexisted during the 17th century. The predominance of the Neapolitan artists is obvious, given the great number of works which arrived in Capodimonte through the expropriation of ecclesiastic goods. However, numerous Emilian, Venetian, and Roman paintings reached Naples with Charles of Bourbon. Among these were the two celebrated panels for the ceiling of the small room of the Hermits, the *Assunzione della Maddalena* (Assumption of Magdalene) and *Gesù servito dagli angeli* (Jesus served by the Angels), decorated by the young Lanfranco, around 1605, in the Palazzetto Farnese in Via Giulia. These canvases are significant for the development of landscape painting of the 17th century, and were obviously considered so important as to be moved from their original location and brought to Rome, Parma and finally Naples. The same happened to the splendid series of six small branches by Carlo Saraceni, which follow the myths inspired by Ovid's *Metamorfosi* (Metamorphosis) in the stories of Icarus, Ariadna and Hermaphroditus. They, too, were important for the history of landscape painting.

The numerous canvases by Schedoni have been praised by all the travellers who have visited the Farnese picture gallery of Capodimonte and by many of the old 19th century guide-books. The most famous, the so called 'Carità piccola' (Small Charity) to distinguish it from the larger version now in the Royal Palace, offers a rare representation of a blind man with open eyes. *Atalanta e Ippomene* (Atalanta and Hippomenes), a mythical transposition from Ovid by Guido Reni, was bought by Domenico Venuti to Rome in 1802. Before then, no other significant work by Guido Reni was included in the paintings coming from Parma. In the very first years of the 19th century Venuti carried out a kind of 'purchase campaign', with the help of Canova and Kauffmann, in order to increase the Bourbon collection. Among the purchases there was also the *Paesaggio* (Landscape) by Lorrain, late work of the master, commissioned by Prince Colonna whose feudal property of Marino is ideally represented as a background for the episode of the nymph Egeria weeping for her spouse Numa Pompilius.

As for the Neapolitan school, the most important work of the collection is the *Flagellazione* (Flagellation) by Caravaggio, in storage for safety reasons, since 1977, from the church of San Domenico Maggiore. Recent X-ray photographs have confirmed the hypothesis that it had been executed at two different times, in 1607 and then in 1609-10, when the artist came back to Naples after his journey to Sicily. The figure of the executioner on the right appears superimposed on the portrait of a man turned towards Christ and shows strong resemblance with the works painted by Merisi in Sicily itself. All the local figurative tradition had to compete with Caravaggio's revolutionary language, especially the early naturalists who reacted to it in different ways while undergoing influences from other new trends. This is the case of Battistello Caracciolo. The references to the *Flagellazione* by Merisi are evident in his *Cristo alla colonna* (Christ at the pillar) bought by a private Neapolitan collection in 1973. Also Carlo Sellitto, who with *Santa Cecilia*, once in the church of Santa Maria della Solitaria, shows his acceptance of the new classicist needs. Caravaggio's influence extended to the more composite experiences of Stanzione, Falcone, Guarino, Artemisia, Gentileschi or Cavallino who, with different tones, mark the passage to a new season of Neapolitan Art. Among the numerous canvases by Cavallino kept in Capodimonte, *Santa Cecilia*, dated 1645, stands out. This is the only signed painting by Cavallino which has been brought back to Naples only recently, after many misfortunes. In fact it was painted for the Church of Sant' Antonio delle Monache a Port'Alba and, already during the first half of the 19th century, passed through more than one private collection. In 1941 it was sold to the Germans with the consent of the Fascist government, and then recovered in 1948 by Rodolfo Siviero and kept in storage in Palazzo Vecchio.

A place of his own is occupied by Ribera with some of his most extraordinary canvases, among which the *Sileno Ebbro* (Drunken Silenus), another of Venuti's purchases, once belonging to the Flemish collector Gaspare Roomer. Also by Ribera are the two famous canvases coming from the church of Trinità delle Monache, *San Gerolamo* (St. Jerome) and *Trinitas Terrestris*, which denote a new pictorial evolution. Unfortunately, some of his works done for the Farnese and even mentioned in the old catalogues have never been found again.

Luca Giordano and Mattia Preti, the two main protagonists of the Neapolitan scene in the second half of the 17th century, appear with great relevance in the catalogue of Capodimonte, to testify to the dense exchange of ideas and painting experiences that occurred between them and which determined the new trend of Neapolitan Baroque painting. Finally, there is a numerous group of still lifes. It includes the oldest works by Luca Forte and the richer and more complex ones of the Recco's and Ruoppolo's generation, but also works by Paolo Porpora and Andrea Belvedere. All of them form a complete picture of the development of one of the most fortunate genres of 17th century Neapolitan painting.

Much less well represented is the presence of 18th century paintings when compared to those of earlier centuries.

The Neapolitan group of painting is centred on the, by now, famous *Ritratto di cavaliere del Real Ordine di San Gennaro* (Portrait of a Knight of the Royal Order of Saint Gennaro), identified with the Prince Tarsia Spinelli, made by Solimena in his late career, and bought in 1981. In addition to this, there are the two portraits by Gaspare Traversi, one donated by Roberto Longhi and the other, dated 1770, which is his last known work. A numerous series of sketches for the decoration with frescos of religious buildings made by Solimena and De Mura, and some meaningful works by De Matteis and Bardellino complete the picture.

Next to these, a relevant series of canvases - commissioned by the sovereigns themselves, very often to non-Neapolitan artists - celebrates significant moments of court life. Such is the case of the two canvases by Giovanni Paolo Pannini which recall the visit of Charles of Bourbon to Pope Benedict XIV after the victory of Velletri in 1744 or, for example, of the imposing official portraits by Anton Raphael Mengs and Angelika Kauffmann. From the Farnese collection, instead, comes the sketch by Sebastiano Ricci for the church of San Vitale in Parma, a presence of relevance to the Venetian school. Also Farnese are a series of numerous views of Venice, uncertainly attributed either to Michele Marieschi or Francesco Albotto, and once believed to be by Canaletto. They were stolen by the French and finally discovered in Rome by Venuti, as usual.

Still in the field of landscapes, this time Neapolitan, a series of pictures - from those by Jacob Philipp Hackert, showing a crystal-clear atmosphere, to the picturesque *Eruzioni del Vesuvio* (Eruptions of the Vesuvius) by Pierre-Jacques Volaire - ideally closes the 18th century survey of the collections of Capodimonte.

Giovanni Lanfranco
Assunzione della Maddalena
(Assumption of Magdalene)
1605 ca.
oil on canvas;
cm 110x78
source: Farnese collection
inventory: Q 341
It belonged to the decoration of the
ceiling of the small room of the Hermits
in the Farnese Palace in via Giulia,
entirely entrusted to the young
Lanfranco in about 1605. With the other
canvases there it was sent to Parma in
1662 and from there to Naples with
Charles of Bourbon. The bird's eye view
is highly impressive and an important
point of reference for the development of
the landscape painting of the 17th
century.

Giovanni Lanfranco
Madonna con il Bambino e i santi
Domenico e Gennaro
(Madonna with Child and the Saints
Domenico and Gennaro)
oil on canvas; cm 300x250
source: Afragola (Naples), church
of the Rosario, stored.

Bartolomeo Schedoni
La Carità
(Charity), 1611
oil on canvas; cm 182x125
source: Farnese collection
inventory: Q 341
Already part of the first Farnese collection at Parma in 1611, the painting is noted among the most famous works by Schedoni for its accentuated realism, its intense expressiveness and the chromatic tone that anticipates the chosen style of the final period of the painter.

Carlo Saraceni
Caduta di Icaro
(Fall of Icarus)
1606-1607
oil on copper; cm 34x54
source: Farnese Collection
inventory: Q 152

Claude Gellée, known as
Claude Lorrain
Paesaggio con la ninfa Egeria
(Landscape with the nymph Egeria)
signed and dated 1669
oil on canvas; cm 155x199
source: Bourbon collection (purchased
1800) inventory: Q 184
The nymph Egeria is weeping over the
death of her spouse Numa Pompilius,
first mythical king of Rome (Ovid,
Metamorfosi).
The ample landscape recalls the lake of
Nemi and the hills of Marino, feudal
property of the Colonna.
The canvas is part of a series of
paintings commissioned by the Prince
Colonna in Lorrain's late career.
It was bought in Rome for the Bourbons
by Domenico Venuti in 1800.

Guido Reni
Atalanta e Ippomene
(Atalanta and Hippomenes)
1620-1625
oil on canvas; cm 191-264
source: Bourbon collection (purchased 1802)
inventory: Q 349

Hippomenes with the help of Venus and the gold apples received from her, manages to defeat the young Atalanta in a race, thus overcoming a trial fatal to all previous pretenders. Reni represents this mythological story stressing its climax in a highly articulated composition also known in a grander version, signed and housed in the Prado museum in Madrid.

112

Michelangelo Merisi, known as il Caravaggio
Flagellazione di Cristo
(The Flagellation of Christ)
1607/1609-10
oil on canvas; cm 266x213
source: Naples, church of San Domenico Magggiore (stored at the Museum of Capodimonte)
This painting comes from the de Franchis Chapel, in the Church of San Domenico Maggiore, where it has been substituted with a copy by Andrea Vaccaro. It was commissioned in May 1607 but completed with the figure of the executioner on the right only around 1609-10, at the time of the artist's second stay in Naples, on his way back from Sicily. It represented a landmark in local painting culture.

Carlo Sellitto
Santa Cecilia
1613
oil on canvas; cm 260x185
source: Naples, Santa Maria della
Solitaria (first inclusion before 1821)
inventory: Q 313

Battistello Caracciolo
Cristo alla colonna
(Christ at the pillar)
1625 ca.
oil on canvas; cm 183x129
source: Naples, Mancini collection
(purchased 1973)
inventory: Q 1780

Jusepe de Ribera
Sileno Ebbro
(Drunken Silenus)
signed and dated 1626
oil on canvas, cm 185x229
source: Bourbon collection
(purchased 1802)
inventory: Q 298
This painting was part of the collection
of the Flemish merchant Gaspare
Roomer, famous collector in 17th
century Naples. The canvas represents -
according to Ovid's tale of the *Fasti*
(Feast) - a feast organised in Bacchus's
honour with satyrs and nymphs, Pan
and Silenus lying in the foreground. It
is one of the most intense peaks of the
early part of Ribera's career, in a phase
when he followed closely the art of
Caravaggio.

116

Jusepe de Ribera
San Girolamo e l'Angelo
del giudizio
(Saint Jerome and the Angel
of Judgement)
1626
oil on canvas; cm 267x164
source: Naples, Trinità delle Monache
inventory: Q 312

Jusepe de Ribera
La Trinità terrestre con i Santi Bruno,
Benedetto, Bernardino e
Bonaventura
(The terrestrial Trinity with the saints
Bruno, Benedetto, Bernardino and
Bonaventura)
signed; 1626-1630 ca.
oil on canvas; cm 393x262
source: Naples, Royal Palace, from the
Church of Trinità delle Monache
inventory: Q 1793

The large composition, completed in the
upper part by an *Eterno Padre* (Eternal
Father), was started in 1626 and
finished before 1630 for the church of
the Trinità delle Monache for which
Ribera also painted, in 1626, *San
Gerolamo e l'Angelo* (Saint Jerome and
the Angel), housed in Capodimonte. It is
a significant example of how de Ribera's
paintings were positively enriched by
Caravaggio's art during the first phase
of his career.

118

Master of the Announcement to the shepherds - name unknown
Annuncio ai pastori
(Announcement to the shepherds)
1625-30
oil on canvas; cm 178x262
source: Naples, San Martino, stored

Massimo Stanzione
Sacrificio di Mosè
(The sacrifice by Moses)
1628-30
oil on canvas; cm 288x225
source: Naples, Lombardi di Cumia
collection (purchased 1953)
inventory: Q 1722

Massimo Stanzione
Adorazione dei pastori
(Adoration of the shepherds)
1645 ca.
oil on canvas; cm 255x 210
source: Naples, church of the Divino
Amore (first inclusion before 1870)
inventory: Q 479

Artemisia Gentileschi
Giuditta e Oloferne
(Judith and Holofernes)
1625-30
oil on canvas; cm 162x126
source: Naples, De Simone collection
(purchased 1827)
inventory: Q 378

Francesco Guarino
Santa Cecilia all'organo
(Saint Cecilia at the organ)
1640 ca.
oil on canvas; cm 124x152
source: Naples; Alfieri collection
(purchased 1845)
inventory: Q 293

Aniello Falcone
Elemosina di Santa Lucia
(The charity of Santa Lucia)
1630 ca.
oil on canvas; cm 75x86
source: Rome, Aldo Briganti collection
(purchased 1966)
inventory: Q 1771

Bernardo Cavallino
Erminia tra i pastori
(Erminia among the shepherds)
1650 ca.
oil on canvas; cm 123x97
source: Naples, Esposito collection
(donation 1938) inv. Q 1717
The subject is taken from
Gerusalemme liberata
by Torquato Tasso.

Bernardo Cavallino
Santa Cecilia in estasi
(Saint Cecilia in ecstasy)
signed and dated 1645
source: Naples, Sant'Antonio delle
Monache
inventory: Q 1795
It is the only dated painting by
Cavallino of great formal elegance and
refined colour. It was once placed on the
high altar of the church of Sant'Antonio
delle Monache near Port'Alba, and then,
in the 19th century, it went to a private
collection. Sold to the Germans in 1941,
it was recovered in 1948 and kept in
Palazzo Vecchio in Florence until it was
sent in 1988 to Capodimonte, where the
preparatory sketch is also kept.

Andrea Vaccaro
Adorazione del vitello d'oro
(Worship of the golden calf)
1650 ca.
oil on canvas; cm 208x260
source: Naples, Colletta collection
(donation 1955)
inventory: Q 1752

Matthias Stomer
Sacra famiglia
(Holy Family)
oil on canvas; cm 152x206
source: Naples, Sant'Efremo Nuovo
(first inclusion from the suppressed
monasteries 1807)
inventory: Q 194

Antonie Van Dyck
Crocifisso
(Crucifix)
oil on canvas; cm 155x111
source: Naples, Sartorio collection
(purchased 1844)
inventory: Q 193

132

Luca Giordano
Nozze di Cana
(The marriage at Cana)
1659-60
oil on canvas, cm 80x100
source: Naples, San Martino
(first inclusion from the suppressed
monasteries 1806)
inventory: Q 267

Luca Giordano
Lucrezia e Tarquinio
(Lucretia and Tarquin)
signed and dated 1663
oil on canvas; cm 160x83
source: d'Avalos collection (donation
1862)

Luca Giordano
Madonna del Rosario
(o del baldacchino)
(Madonna of the Rosary - or of the
canopy) 1686 ca.
oil on canvas; cm 430x240
source: Naples, Santo Spirito di Palazzo
(first inclusion from the suppressed
monasteries after 1816)
inventory: Q.268
The monumental composition clearly

derives its origin from sculptural motifs
both in its whole conception and in the
particular such as the angels that are
holding the canopy or the harmony and
roundness of the putti (small boys) that
remind one of Bernini. It is one of the
most successful works in Giordano's vast
production, with affinity to the work of
Gaulli, one of his contemporaries. He
was also interested in transposing, on a
pictorial level, Bernini's achievements.

Luca Forte
Natura morta con pere e mele
(Still life with pears and apples)
1640 ca.
oil on canvas, cm 26x35
source: Naples, Museum Duca di
Martina, stored.

Luca Forte
Natura morta con ciliege, fragole e frutti
(Still life with cherries, strawberries and fruit), 1640 ca.
oil on canvas; cm 26x35
source: Naples, Museum Duca di
Martina, stored.

Giovan Battista Recco
Interno di cucina
(Kitchen interior)
1650 ca.
oil on canvas; cm 128x140
source: Naples, Baratti collection
(purchased 1972)
inventory: Q 1776

Giuseppe Recco
Pesci
(Fish)
1680 ca.
oil on canvas; cm 157x203
source: Naples, Errico Frascione
collection (donation 1921)
inventory: Q 303

Giovan Battista Ruoppolo
Natura morta con ortaggi
(Still life with vegetables)
1650 ca.
oil on canvas, cm 50x76
source: not ascertained (before 1930)
inventory: Q 1217

Paolo Porpora
Fiori con coppa di cristallo
(Flowers with crystal bowl)
1655 ca.
oil on canvas; cm 148x113
source: not ascertained
(before 1930)
inventory: Q 972

Francesco Solimena
Ritratto del Principe Tarsia Spinelli in abiti da Cavaliere del Reale Ordine di San Gennaro
(Portrait of the Prince Tarsia Spinelli dressed as a knight of the Royal Order of Saint Gennaro), 1741 ca.
oil on canvas; cm 250x168
source: Naples, Enrico Gaetani collection (purchased 1981)
inventory: 1787

It is a superb work of the last period of the career of the artist, dated around 1741 representing Ferdinando Vincenzo Spinelli, prince of Tarsia, famous collector and figure of great relevance at the court of Charles of Bourbon. The Prince of Tarsia was among the first aristocrats to be conferred this title by the king who founded the order in 1738.

Francesco Solimena
Enea e Didone
(Aeneas and Dido)
1739-41 ca.
oil on canvas; cm 435x340
source: Naples, Palazzo Tarsia Spinelli
(purchased 1961)
inventory: S. M. 1734
Aeneas meets Dido and offers her gifts

while Cupid, in the guise of Ascanio, is
already near the queen in order to
favour her falling in love. It is a work of
the final part of Solimena's career, a
kind of compendium of all his most
successful pictorial and compositional
ideas, re-utilised with renewed vigour by
the artist in his late career obtaining
impressive results.

Francesco De Mura
San Benedetto accoglie Totila
(Saint Benedict welcomes Totila)
1710 ca.
source: Naples, Pio Monte della
Misericordia, legacy de Mura
(purchased 1907)
inventory: Q 218
It is a preparatory sketch for the frescos
that embellish the vault of the
Neapolitan church of Santi Severino e
Sossio.
De Mura worked at the decoration of the
entire church on several occasions
between 1738 and 1746, starting from
the vault, where he clearly followed the
style of Solimena.
It was purchased by the Museum in
1907, together with two more sketches of
the same series.

142

Gaspare Traversi
Ritratto di canonico
(Portrait of a canon)
signed 1770
oil on canvas; cm 77x63
source: New York, Ganz collection
(purchased 1989)
inventory: Q 1788
It is the last known work of the artist, a
significant example of a great portrait
painting technique that combines great
formal rigour and psychological insight.

Anton Raphael Mengs
Ritratto di Ferdinando IV fanciullo
(Portrait of Ferdinand IV as a child)
1760 ca.
oil on canvas; cm 180x126
source: Bourbon collection
inventory: Q.207
The portrait of the young king at the age of nine was painted by Mengs, just then arrived at the Neapolitan court. Special effects are created by the matching of colours together with the richness of details, and the surrounding setting that stresses the role and the importance of the young king, portrayed in spite of his youth.

Angelica Kauffman
La famiglia di Ferdinando
di Borbone
(The family of Ferdinand of Bourbon)
1783
oil on canvas; cm 300x425
source: Bourbon collection
inventory: O.A. 6557

Giovanni Paolo Pannini
Carlo III di Borbone visita il Papa Benedetto XIV nella coffee-house del Quirinale
(Charles III of Bourbon visits Pope Benedict XIV in the coffee-house of the Quirinale)
1746
oil on canvas; cm 121x171
source: Bourbon collection

inventory: Q 205
It was commissioned, together with a *pendant*, by Charles of Bourbon to commemorate a visit made to the Pope after the victory at Velletri against the Austrians in 1744. The refined mundane character of the composition is exalted by the rich variety of people in positions and attitudes of acute realism and great sensitivity.

Jacob Philip Hackert
Ferdinando IV a caccia di folaghe sul lago Fusaro
(Ferdinand IV hunting coots on lake Fusaro), 1783
oil on canvas; cm 141x219
source: Bourbon collection
inventory: OA 7422

Pierre- Jacques-Antoine Volaire
Eruzione del Vesuvio
(Eruption of Vesuvius)
signed and dated 1782
oil on canvas, cm 130x229
source: d'Avalos collection
(donation 1862)
inventory: d'Avalos 22

Michele Marieschi (attr.)
*Veduta di Venezia con la chiesa
della Salute*
(View of Venice with the chiesa
della Salute)
oil on canvas, cm 62x97
source: Farnese collection
Inv Q 819

148

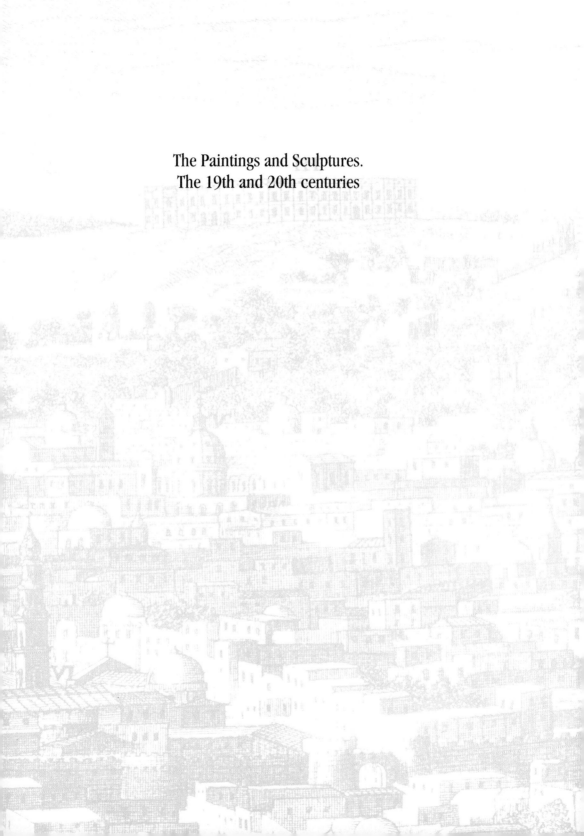

The Paintings and Sculptures.
The 19th and 20th centuries

In the first half of the 19th century, in Naples as in the rest of Europe, two different artistic trends developed. On the one hand, the neo-classic current established itself also thanks to the notable archaeological discoveries in the areas of both Pozzuoli (the Puteolan) and Vesuvius. On the other hand Romantic sensitivity emerged on the wave of natural beauty contemplated with vibrant emotion. Furthermore, the rich cultural contribution of the numerous foreign artists in Naples in those years added to the development of figurative art.

The large canvases of the 19th century arrived in Capodimonte at that time as gifts, court purchases or as paintings presented in the hope of obtaining a grant from the court. They were mainly on mythological or historical subjects, and were kept and arranged, more as furnishings than as real museum fittings, by the official painter Tommaso De Vivo. As far as the landscape is concerned we must underline the innovative language proposed by Anton Sminck Pitloo (b. Arnhem 1791- d. Naples 1837), the active and inspired teacher of that subject at the Academy, and by Giacinto Gigante (b. Naples 1806 - d.1876). They were both sensitive interpreters of the reality no longer seen as a memory-image but as the artist's emotional response to nature.

The official court painter Gabriele Smargiassi (b. Vasto 1798 - d. 1889) held the same Chair immediately after Pitloo. However, owing to his artistic temperament which was more inclined to official illustration, there was a fall in vitality. In spite of this, the painters of the so called Posillipo School formed a group rich in important names and works. With reference to the Academy, it is important to note that Giuseppe (b. Lanciano 1812 - d. Paris 1888) and Filippo Palizzi (b. Vasto 1818 - d. Naples 1899) soon abandoned their apprenticeship because of their strongly held dissatisfaction. Filippo joined the new scholastic Institute of Applied Arts, whereas Giuseppe was one of the first Neapolitan artists to live in France (in Barbizon), where he discovered a drive towards a more modern method of landscape painting.

Other stimuli came from the Tuscan area, especially from the movement of the Macchiaioli imported to Naples by Adriano Cecioni (b. Vagnia 1836- d. Florence 1886), theorist of the movement, as well as sensitive artist, who contributed to the reinforcement of the revolutionary theory intrinsic to the Resina School. In this close group the work of masters of great sensitivity, such as Marco De Gregorio (b. Resina 1829 - d. Naples 1875) and Federico Rossano (b. Naples 1835 - d. 1915) was not, at that time, very much appreciated and the experience ended there, in spite of the substantial artistic programme. Only Giuseppe De Nittis (b. Barletta 1846 - d. Saint-Germain en Laye 1884), was very successful, probably because less committed to social problems.

Domenico Morelli (b. Naples 1823 - d. 1901), already oriented in 1855 towards the new socio-romantic sensitivity with *Gli Iconoclasti* (The Iconoclasts), assumed a position of his own although he sometimes seemed to tend towards the "illustration" typical of the historical novel, or the orientalism, then fashionable, or the trial of some valid expressive techniques such as in the *Dama col ventaglio* (Lady with fan). The second half of the 19th century was characterised by an ensemble of painters. These painters, from Mancini to Toma, from Altamura to Netti, from Cammarano to Patini, from Michetti to Migliaro, although with changing languages and personalities, represented intensively different effective aspects and features of the life in Naples. With them Vincenzo Gemito (b. Naples 1852 - d. 1929) was a lively interpreter of the popular tradition, full of vibrant ideas borrowed from the Hellenistic world which emerged, in various ways, during his long career.

In conclusion, after the Unification of Italy, since many Royal Palaces were put to a different use, it was thought to use Capodimonte as a picture gallery «gathering the numerous precious modern works of sculpture and painting existing in these southern Royal Palaces». The gentleman Annibale Sacco was entrusted with this for about twenty years from 1864, and was assisted in his museum choices by Domenico Morelli and Federico Maldarelli (A. Sacco, *Notizie sul palazzo di Capodimonte* - Information on the palace of Capodimonte, 1884).

Sacco changed the arrangement of the works several times according to the purchases, gifts or transfers to (or from) other Royal Palaces. On the subject of these arrangements the *Guida alla pinacoteca reale di Capodimonte* (Guide to the picture gallery of Capodimonte), published in 1887, by the famous painter Gonsalvo Carelli, can be useful in spite of its limitations.

After more than half a century of indifference to the conditions of the 19th century gallery, merit must be given to Bruno Molajoli who, in 1957, managed to organise it again, adding the donation of the Rotondo brothers (now in San Martino) to a choice of works coming from the Bourbon collection and from the post Unitarian one.

In the same year the outstanding collection of the «commendatore» Alfonso Marino arrived at the Museum, and, after a while, arrived the temporary deposit of the 19th century works, owned by the Banco di Napoli. In 1962, 13 paintings by Gioacchino Toma, bequeathed by his son Gustavo, were added, and then in 1965 a series of works by foreign painters from the collection of the Princess Margherita Soulier di Marsiconovo.

In 1972 the considerable Astarita donation arrived with some oils and hundreds of drawings and paintings on paper executed by Giacinto Gigante.

In 1986 the important painting of the divisionist period by Giacomo Balla was donated to the museum. In 1993, the procedures for the acceptance of the important donation of some works by Vincenzo Gemito from his youngest niece were begun.

Louis Lemasle
*Il matrimonio della Principessa
Maria Carolina di Borbone col Duca
di Berry*
(The wedding of the Princess Maria
Carolina of Bourbon with the Duke of
Berry), signed and dated 1822-23
oil on canvas; cm 175x238

source: Bourbon collection
inventory: 176 O.A.
The wedding here represented was
celebrated by proxy on 24th April 1816
in the Chapel of the Royal Palace in
Naples, and the Duke of Berry for the
occasion was represented by Prince
Leopold of Bourbon.

152

Vincenzo Camuccini
L'uccisione di Giulio Cesare
(The murder of Julius Caesar)
1793-1806 ca.
oil on paper laid down on a small
board; cm 24x38
source: Redaelli collection (purchased
1965)
inventory: 1741 Q.

Alexandre Dunouy
Napoli da Portici
(Naples seen from Portici)
signed and dated 1814
oil on canvas cm 130x182
source: Bourbon collection
inventory: 1394 O.A.

Johann Christian Dahl
La Real Casina di Quisisana
(The Royal House of Quisisana)
signed and dated 1820
oil on canvas; cm 93x136.5
source: Princes of Denmark
(donation 1820),

inventory: 1388 O.A.
The painter was sent to Naples for a few
months by Prince Friederick of
Denmark to do the painting to be given
to King Ferdinand I, as a token of
gratitude for the hospitality received in
the House of Quisisana.

Anton Sminck Pitloo
I templi di Paestum
(The temples of Paestum)
1824-25 ca.
oil on canvas, cm 60x86
source: Bourbon collection
inventory: 112 O.A.
The painting can be attributed to the first years of the Flemish painter's Italian stay, when he devoted himself to the naturalistic representation of classic monuments, moreover without emphasis or rhetoric.
Pitloo had already tended towards a pictorial language free from academic schemes. Here we can still see the classicist basis of his art expressed though in a colloquial style.

156

Anton Sminck Pitloo
Il boschetto Francavilla al Chiatamone
(Francavilla thicket at the Chiatamone)
1823-24 ca.
oil on canvas; cm 44x75
source: Banco di Napoli collection;
(stored)

Giacinto Gigante
La Marinella
1855 ca.
signed
pencil and watercolour on paper;
mm 348x530
source: Banco di Napoli collection
(stored)

Giacinto Gigante
*La costiera d'Amalfi con mare in
tempesta*
(Amalfi coast with stormy sea)
1837 ca.
signed
oil on canvas; cm 28.5x40.5
source: acquired before 1874
inventory: 40 O.A.

158

Giacinto Gigante
*La Cappella del Tesoro nel Duomo
di Napoli*
(The Chapel of Treasure in the
Cathedral of Naples)
signed and dated 1863
watercolour on paper; mm 720x525
source: purchased by King Vittorio
Emanuele II (1863)
inventory: 134 P.S.
The solemn ceremony on the occasion
of the melting of the blood of Saint
Gennaro, which happens twice a year
(in May and in September) in the
Treasure Chapel, is here represented.
The painting, directly commissioned
and purchased by the King is important
for Gigante's expressive research. The
particular use of colour on paper
permits the effective glare of the
candlelights on the silvers and the
bronzes which decorate the chapel.

Domenico Morelli
Gli Iconoclasti
(The Iconoclasts)
signed and dated 1855
oil on canvas; cm 257x212
source: acquired before 1860
inventory: 74 P.S.

160

Domenico Morelli
Dama con ventaglio
(Lady with fan)
signed and dated 1873
oil on canvas; cm 111x76.5
source: Banco di Napoli collection
(stored)
In this painting, which used to be part

of the collection of the Marquis Doria
and Duke of Eboli, can be seen the
influence of Luminism as the colours
assume an unusual richness and
lightness.
The variations of the white of the fabrics
in the lower part of the painting assume
special importance.

Marco de Gregorio
Veduta di Casacalenda
(View of Casacalenda)
1863-67 ca.
oil on canvas; cm 67x84
source: Marino collection
(donation 1957)
inventory: 7700 O.A.

Giovanni Fattori
Soldato a cavallo
(Soldier on horseback)
1870 ca.; signed
oil on panel; cm 36.5x21
source: Cenzato collection
(donation 1969)

inventory: 8308 O. A.
The light cavalryman shows a strong
vigour in his physical configuration.
A special energy appears in the hint of
movement and in the front position of
the figure engaged in the action.

Giuseppe de Nittis
La traversata degli Appennini
(The crossing of the Appenines)
signed and dated 1867
oil on canvas; cm 44x76
source: purchased by King Vittorio
Emanuele II (1867)
inventory: 61 P. S.

Michele Cammarano
Ozio e lavoro
(Idleness and work)
1862-63 ca.
oil on canvas, cm 60x118
source: purchased by King Vittorio
Emanuele II (1863)
inventory: 9 P. S.

164

Michele Cammarano
I legnaiuoli
(The woodcutters)
1878 ca.
oil on canvas; cm 30x45
source: Banco di Napoli collection
(temporarily stored)

Nicola Palizzi
Rivista militare al Campo di Marte
(Military review on parade ground)
signed and dated 1857
oil on canvas; cm 20x27
source: Marino collection
(donation 1957)
inventory: 7643 O. A.

Filippo Palizzi
Studio per la Gita a Cava
(Study for the Trip to Cava)
signed and dated 1881
oil on canvas; cm 24x38
source: Marino collection
(donation 1957)
inventory: 7633 O. A.
Sketch for a painting in private collection. The unquestionable novelty both of the pictorial and compositional language compared to the paintings usually done by the illustrious artist are to be pointed out.
In spite of the fact that the scene takes place in the open air, the main elements in the painting are the portraits of the characters and the sensitivity towards the light that gives off different shades of colour in the undergrowth.
The overhanging foliage of the trees, and the sky are only to be imagined. There are clear references to the French painting of his times, learned from his brother Giuseppe, who lived for a long time in Barbizon.

Francesco Netti
La sortie du bal
(Leaving after the ball)
signed and dated 1872
oil on canvas; cm 46x56
source: Morisani collection
(donation 1978)
inventory: 8340 O.A.

Teofilo Patini
Studio per le bestie da soma
(Study for the Beasts of burden)
1885 ca., signed
oil on canvas; cm 31x40
source: Marino collection
(donation 1957)
inventory: 7677 O.A.

Gioacchino Toma
Luisa Sanfelice in carcere
(Luisa Sanfelice in jail)
signed and dated 1874
oil on canvas; cm 63x79
source: Gualtieri collection
(purchased 1970)
inventory: 7798 O. A.
Here the Neapolitan noblewoman,
condemned to death during the
Bourbon Restoration after the
unsuccessful Republic of 1799, is
depicted. The character is busy sewing
the layette for the child to be born. The
intention, typical of the artist, is
evidently to represent the drama of a
woman linked to everyday life more
than to a political commitment. There
are also some sketches and a second
draft made in 1877.

Gioacchino Toma
Il tatuaggio dei camorristi
(The tattooing of the 'camorristi'
Neapolitan criminals)
1888-90 ca.
oil on canvas; cm 88x130
source: Toma collection
(donation 1960)
inventory: 7723 O.A.

Antonio Mancini
Autoritratto
(Self-portrait)
dated 1882
red-ochre on drawing paper
mm 580x460
source: purchased by King Umberto I
(1882)
inventory: 305 P. S.

172

Francesco Paolo Michetti
Autoritratto
(Self-portrait)
1895 ca., signed
oil on canvas; cm 49x34
source: Marino collection
(donation 1957)
inventory: 7688 O. A.

Vincenzo Gemito
La zingara
(The Gypsy girl)
signed and dated 1885
pencil and watercolour with white lead
relief on paper; mm 470x300
source: Banco di Napoli collection
(stored)

Vincenzo Gemito
Autoritratto
(Self-portrait)
signed and dated 1914
pencil on parchment; mm 640x510
source: Banco di Napoli collection
(stored)

Francesco Paolo Michetti
La Processione del Venerdì Santo
(The Procession of 'Holy' Friday)
signed and dated 1895
pastel charcoal and watercolour on
paper; mm 850x920
source: Cenzato collection
(donation 1969)
inventory: 8295 O. A.

Antonio Mancini
Ritratto con ventaglio
(Portrait with fan)
signed and dated 1922
oil on canvas; cm 70x60
source: Marino collection
(donation 1957)
inventory: 7685 O. A.

Vincenzo Migliaro
San Biagio dei Librai
signed and dated 1928
oil on canvas; cm 56x51
source: Marino collection
(donation 1957)
inventory: 7692 O. A.
Via San Biagio dei Librai is a street in
Naples famous for its many bookshops.

Giovanni Boldini
Strillone parigino
(Parisian newspaper seller)
1880 ca., signed
oil on panel; cm 47x29
source: Marino collection
(donation 1957)
inventory: 7681 O. A.
Boldini tries his hand at a theme
unusual for him, where every element of
the painting tends towards a social
characterisation. On the one hand, the
cue comes from the marked realism of
the famous French artists Daumier and
Courbet, while the overall construction
of the character, on the other hand,
refers to the refined figures of the world
of Boldini.

Giovanni Boldini
La Passeggiata nel Parco
(Walk in the park)
1884 ca.
signed
oil on canvas; cm 55x44
source: Marino collection
(donation 1957)
inventory: 7663 O. A

This picture produces a happy symbiosis between a female portrait and the representation of an autumnal landscape. The woman's face, almost porcelain like, is typical of Boldini's representation of women. It stands out from the rest of the painting which is expressed with a well organised mode of French origin.

Gaetano Previati
Lo Sposalizio
(The Wedding)
1895-96 ca.
oil on canvas; cm 25x40
source: Marino collection
(donation 1957)
inventory: 7659 O. A.

Giuseppe Pellizza da Volpedo
Il Prato
(The lawn)
signed and dated 1897
oil on panel, cm 22x35
source: Marino collection
(donation 1957)
inventory: 7661 O. A.

In spite of the influence of divisionism, the landscape in this painting still retains naturalistic features. The painting is dedicated to the Neapolitan painter Casciaro, a friend of the artist. The work belonged to his collection before passing to the Marino's.

Giacomo Balla
La famiglia Carelli
(The Carelli family)
signed; 1901-02
oil on canvas; cm 100x75.5
source: Carelli collection
(donation 1986)
inventory: 8376 O. A.
It was commissioned as a portrait of Lady Carelli, but Balla wanted to include in the frame her husband and their young daughter Libera, who was to become a famous scholar and a sensitive Neapolitan poetess. The work is highly representative of the so called 'portrait painting' period, just before the futuristic phase which started about 1910. This work shows the maturity in expression reached by the author after his Turinese, Roman and Parisian experiences.

182

Andy Warhol
Vesuvius
1985
acrylic on canvas; cm 240x300
source: donation of Lucio Amelio
(1993)
inventory: Q 1794
The painting was done on the occasion
of the exhibition *Vesuvius by Warhol*,
held in 1985 in the Museum of
Capodimonte in Naples. The American
artist wanted to render homage to the
most famous and recurrent among the
themes of the Parthenopean landscape,
the erupting Vesuvius. The image of the
Volcano, repeated in series, is
transformed into an icon of
communication.

Bertel Thorwaldsen
La Notte
(The Night), 1815, signed
marble bas-relief; diam. cm 77
source: Bourbon collection

inventory: 10815 A. M.
It is an autographed replica (1835),
among the numerous reproductions of
this important relief, done by
Thorwaldsen in his study in Rome.

Vincenzo Gemito
Il giocatore
(The player)
1867-68 ca.
bronzed plaster, h. cm 64
source: purchased by King Vittorio
Emanuele II (1868)
inventory: 203 P.S.

The work, purchased by the king in
1868, was never cast in bronze. It was
seriously damaged during the Second
World War, but repaired with an
accurate restoration in the fifties.
It is proof of the first period of Gemito's
studies on the «Neapolitan urchins».

186

Vincenzo Gemito
Il fiociniere
(The harpooner)
signed and dated 1872
terracotta, h. cm 36
source: Banco di Napoli collection
(stored)

Giacomo Ginotti
L'emancipazione della schiavitù
(The emancipation from slavery)
signed and dated 1877
marble, h. cm 150
source: purchased by King Vittorio
Emanuele II (1877)
inventory: 186 P.S.

Vincenzo Gemito
Ritratto di Raffaele Viviani
(Portrait of Raffaele Viviani)
signed and dated 1926
terracotta, h. cm 47

source: Viviani collection
(donation 1975)
inventory: 1444
Viviani was a famous Neapolitan actor
and writer of comedies.

189

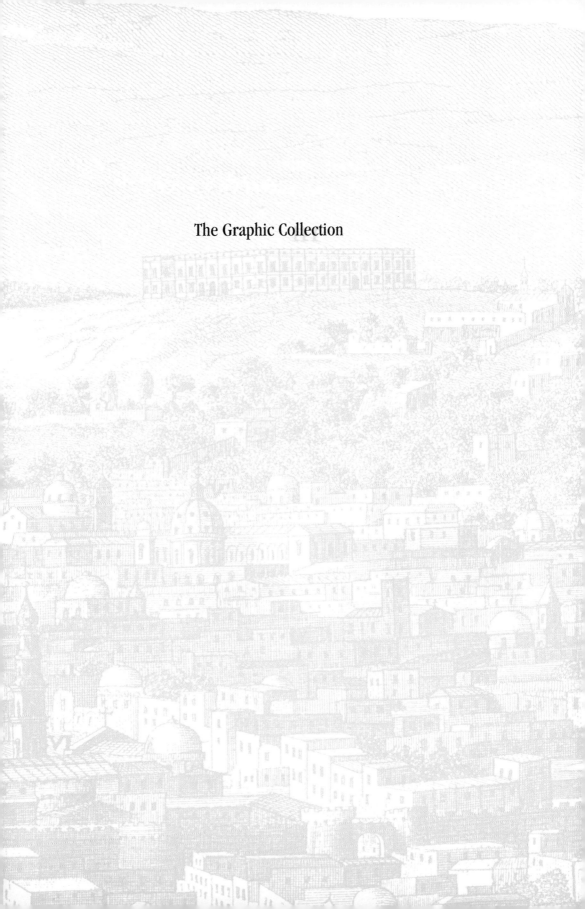

The Graphic Collection

The graphic collection of Capodimonte is basically a reflection of the historical events of the museum. It can be divided in different groups, including altogether 2,500 sheets (drawings and watercolours), and slightly more than 22,000 prints.

The oldest group is made up of 52 drawings belonging to the collections of Casa Farnese inherited by Charles of Bourbon and transferred from Parma to Naples after 1734. Originally more substantial, it was considerably reduced before the passage to the southern capital. Other sheets of the same collection have been identified, for example, at the Louvre Museum, the British Museum and the Windsor Royal Collections. The collection was initially housed at the Palazzo Farnese in Rome and from 1662 at the Palazzo del Giardino in Parma. In Naples it was first placed, together with the collection of pictures, the library and the collection of medals, in some rooms on the piano nobile of the new Royal Palace of Capodimonte and after that, since the beginning of the last century, in the seat of the Royal Bourbon Museum in the Palazzo dei Regi Studi. The most famous and precious examples of this Farnese group are certainly the three, recently restored, 'cartoons' (draft sketches). One is by Michelangelo with details of the frescos in the Cappella Paolina in the Vatican, one by Raffaello for the *Mosè davanti al roveto ardente* (Moses in front of the burning bush) in the vault of Eliodoro's Room in the Vatican, and one by an anonymous follower of Michelangelo's style for the *Venere con Cupido* (Venus with Cupid), from a lost original of Michelangelo himself. They belonged, together with other sheets of the same collection, among which is a rare drawing by Sofonisba Anguissola of a *Fanciullo morso da un gambero* (Child bitten by a prawn), to the rich collection of art and antiquities donated by Fulvio Orsini to Cardinal Odoardo Farnese in 1600. Orsini was a famous scholar and bibliophile in the service first, of Ranuccio, and then of Alessandro Farnese in Rome. Included in the Farnese collection, besides a cartoon by Raffaello representing the *Madonna del Divino Amore* (Madonna of the Divine Love), there are some important drawings which unfortunately have reached us in terrible conditions because of past tampering and prolonged exposure to the sun. Worthy of mention are those coming mainly from the Parmesan school (those of Parmigianino, Mazzola Bedoli and Bertoja), the Bolognese school (Annibale Carracci) and Roman school (Taddeo and Federico Zuccari). They represent a selection of masters also present in the painting collection, and confirm a substantial homogeneous taste, mainly in style between Mannerism and Classicism adopted in the Emilian area.

The original Farnese collection had partially been plundered by the French in 1799 and temporarily transferred to Rome. Even the two cartoons by Michelangelo and Raffaello were packed but not dispatched. It was put together, between the 18th and 19th centuries, after the transfer from Capodimonte to the Royal Bourbon Museum, with 1,024 more sheets by Emilian (from Agostino Carracci to Guercino), Florentine (Andrea del Sarto and Pontormo), Genoese (Cambiaso), Venetian (Tintoretto and Palma the Younger) and French (Callot) authors, thanks to purchases made according to the will of Ferdinand I. Of this 'Bourbon' group the most significant set of drawings, both with regard to quantity and to their connections with the history of painting in Naples at the beginning of the 17th century, is made up of 138 sheets by Giovanni Lanfranco (not all autographed). These document widely the creative genesis of the cycles of frescos painted by Lanfranco, between 1635 and 1646, for various Neapolitan churches (from Gesù Nuovo to San Martino, from Santi Apostoli to the Treasure of Saint Gennaro).

With Stefano Borgia's collection, given to the Bourbon Museum in 1817, were 86 rare paintings done in India (watercolours and drawings with a mixed technique) which became part of the graphic section. However, even more important had been the purchase, on behalf of the king, of the famous collection of drawings and prints belonging to the Trentine Count Carlo Firmian, already Minister Plenipotentiary of Austria and Milan and, from 1754 to 1758, Imperial Ambassador in Naples. This part of the collection had been auctioned, together with paintings, tapestries, medals and a precious library, the year after the eminent collector's death, to pay off the substantial debts contracted in his lifetime. It included no less than 20,571 engravings and drawings collected in 231 volumes. It was purchased for Ferdinand of Bourbon's private Royal Library and in 1860 it had become part of the personal property of the House of Savoy. Since 1864 it had been permanently assigned to the National Museum of Naples as a gift from Vittorio Emanuele II. The collection of prints, divided into 277 volumes, includes remarkable engravings of the Northern School. Among them are Dürer, present with the famous illustrations of the *Apocalisse* (Apocalypse), the *Grande Passione* (Great Passion), the *Vita della Vergine* (Life of the Virgin), and the *Piccola Passione* (Small Passion), *La grande Fortuna* (The great Fortune), *Melencolia* (Melancholy), *Il Cavaliere* (The Knight), the *Morte e il Diavolo* (Death and the Devil), the *Ritratto dell'imperatore Massimiliano I* (Portrait of the Emperor Maximilian I), and the 'little masters of Nurimberg', with images of Altdorfer, Aldegrever, the Beham brothers and Hans Baldung Grien. Finally, there are some works by the great Dutchmen, such as Luca from Leyda and Rembrandt and outstanding examples of engraving technique, regarding both original works and reproductions (from Michelangelo to Raffaello, from Titian to Rubens). Particularly noteworthy is a series of 50 engravings (burin) of an anonymous master from Ferrara in 1465, with the representation of the tarot cards wrongly indicated as 'Mantegna's' tarot cards. Among the drawings, some of them already attributed to famous authors, are certainly interesting those of Pietro di Cosimo, Fra' Bartolomeo, Rembrandt, Ribera, Mattia Preti or other masters of Neapolitan, Venetian and Lumbard Schools between the 16th and 17th centuries.

Another considerable group, whose origin has not yet been identified (but it is likely to be another Bourbon purchase), is made up of numerous sheets with architectural drawings, once collected in a volume, and now separately mounted in *passepartout*. They are mostly studies and projects by Ferdinando Sanfelice. This famous architect, painter, scenographer and designer of ephemeral sumptuous decorations for feasts and public ceremonies had been trained at Solimena's school and was, together with Domenico Antonio Vaccaro, among the great representatives of the Neapolitan rococò. In 1957 even the collection of prints and drawings was transferred from the National Museum to the re-structured Museum of Capodimonte and arranged in the narrow space of the two rooms on the piano

nobile. Since then further additions to the 18th and 19th century collection have taken place, thanks only to some donations of famous and generous private citizens, among whom Angelo and Mario Astarita are worthy of special mention. In fact, in 1970 they donated the entire collection of no less than 419 drawings, watercolours and oils by Giacinto Gigante and other representatives of the famous Posillipo School. Thus, a collection of pictorial documents, fundamental to the understanding of this important chapter of landscape painting in Naples during the Romantic Age, was created. Still with reference to the Neapolitan 19th century, it is important to mention the selection of drawings by Neapolitan painters and sculptors, in particular those by Domenico Morelli and by Vincenzo Gemito, bought from the lawyer Gabriele Consolatio in 1954. These belonged to the art collections of the Banco di Napoli which, since 1960, have been exhibited at Capodimonte.

Three silver plates of Farnese origin belonging to the Cardinal Odoardo Farnese's personal collection have to be linked to the prints and drawings collection. One was engraved by Annibale Carracci with the *Sileno ebbro* (Drunken Silenus), the other by Francesco Villamena with the same subject, and the third by an anonymous artist who copied Agostino Carracci's version of the *Cristo di Caprarola* (Christ of Caprarola) by Annibale. The first two were originally used also as table ornaments (respectively as saucers and bread dish), but they were all used as print moulds.

In the new arrangement of Farnese paintings and items, on the first floor of the Museum, a large space in two corner halls has been given to the presentation of some of the most famous drawings of Casa Farnese, in particular the three cartoons by Michelangelo, Raffaello and by the School of Michelangelo. The entire department of the Study of Drawings and Prints has been recently transferred to the rooms in the southern wing of the Palace. On the ground floor, there are ten halls equipped for temporary exhibitions. On the mezzanine are study halls, preservation laboratories and elements in rotation of the permanent collection, besides a restoration workshop. The restoration of the rooms, already used as offices and workshops, started in 1988, following a project by Ezio De Felice and with funding both ministerial and of

Fra' Bartolomeo
Figura avanzante, il profilo a destra,
in atto di leggere
(Advancing figure, profile to the right,
in the act of reading)
1499
black pencil, white lead on white
watercolour paper;
mm 290x182

source: Farnese collection
inventory: 1028
It is the preparatory study for the
prophet Elijah in the fresco of the
Giudizio Universale (the Last
Judgement) painted in 1499 for the
Hospital of Santa Maria Nuova of
Florence (now at the museum of
San Marco).

194   the Agency for Southern Italy. The new arrangement became necessary to offer adequate solutions to the new needs of a public more and more interested in the different aspects of ancient, modern and contemporary graphic art. The innovative changes will permit more effective conservation of the original material, more comfortable conditions for study and will generally help to make best use of the whole collection.

Piero di Cosimo
Testa femminile di profilo
(Female head in profile)
1500-1510
sepia and ink on brownish paper
mm 209x168
source: Firmian collection
inventory: 106

Raffaello Sanzio
Mosè innanzi al roveto ardente
(Moses in front of the burning Bush)
1514 ca.
charcoal and white lead relief on 23
sheets of paper. Pierced edges for
pounching;
mm 1400x1380
source: Farnese collection
inventory: I.G.M.N. 86653

It is a fragment of the preparatory
cartoon used for the Moses painted in
fresco in one of four sections of the vault
in the Room of Eliodoro in the Vatican,
on which work started in 1511 and
ended in 1514. The cartoon first
belonged to Fulvio Orsi, librarian of the
Farnese who, in 1600, bequeathed his
important art collection to cardinal
Odoardo.

Andrea del Sarto
Studi di figura genuflessa volta a sinistra (recto)
(Studies on a kneeling figure turned towards left), 1528-30
red-ochre and black pencil,
mm 265x205
source: Bourbon collection
inventory: 1027
It is the study, improved at various stages, of the pose of Saint Catherine of Alessandria in the altar-piece with the *Madonna in gloria e quattro santi* (Madonna in glory and four saints). It was done between 1528 and 1530 but left unfinished, for the church of San Fedele di Poppi, and now in the Pitti Palace. It was completed in 1540 by Vincenzo Fornario, known as Morgante Bonilli da Poppi.

198

Michelangelo (attr.)
Venere e Amore
(Venus and Cupid)
1535 ca.
charcoal, mm 1310x1840
source: Farnese collection
inventory: 86654
The work was created by Michelangelo
on a cartoon executed in 1532-34 for his
friend Bartolomeo Bettini, and there are
several copies and versions of the same
work. The Neapolitan cartoon, already
attributed to the master in the inventory
of the Orsini collection, then donated to
Odoardo Farnese, was therefore simply
considered as a copy and then attributed
to Bronzino, Alessandro Allori and the
School of the Pontormo. The identical
subject is reproduced in a panel of the
same size, housed in the Neapolitan
museum and belonging to the same
collection. This latter has been attributed,
with reservations, to the Northern painter
Hendrik van der Broecke.

Girolamo Mazzola Bedoli
Uomo seduto con violoncello entro una nicchia, in alto orchestra d'angeli
(Man sitting in a corner with a cello, choir of angels above)
1542 ca.
red-ochre and white lead on white paper; mm 207x140
source: Farnese collection
inventory: 649

The drawing is datable to a very early phase of Bedoli's career, full of refined tones typical of Coreggio and Parmigianino. It could be the elaborated study, accurate in its execution and technique, for the decoration of the small doors of the organ in San Giovanni Evangelista in Parma. In fact, records of payment for the execution of this work go back to 1546.

Parmigianino
Cupido saettante
(Cupid shooting his arrows)
1527-1530
pen-and-ink on white paper,
mm 182x132
source: Farnese collection
inventory: 1037

A brilliant invention on the theme of
Cupid which is often to be found in the
graphic production of Parmigianino, on
papers all datable around the Bolognese
period, between 1527 to 1530.
Because of the technique used this is
considered a preparatory study for an
engraving or a trial for a 'chiaroscuro'.

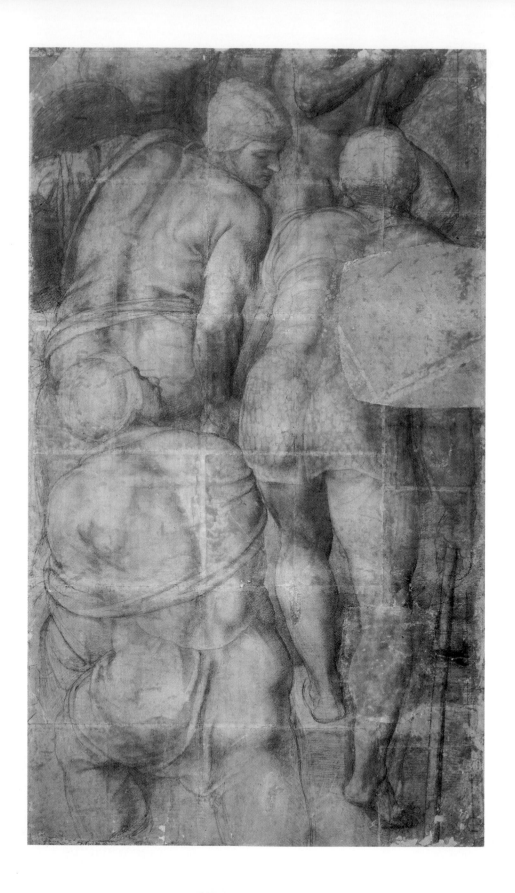

Michelangelo Buonarroti
Gruppo di armigeri
(Group of warriors)
1546 ca.
charcoal on 19 sheets of royal Bolognese paper. Pierced edges for the pounching; mm 2630x1560
source: Farnese collection
inventory: IGMN 86687
It is a fragment of the preparatory cartoon which Michelangelo used to trace on the wall the drawing of the three life-sized figures, seen from the back, that appear in the fresco of *La Crocifissione di San Pietro* (The Crucifixion of Saint Peter) in the Paolina Chapel in the Vatican. The execution of the work can be dated around 1546, when Michelangelo, by then a septuagenarian, achieved an extreme simplicity in his artistic language.

Jacopo Zanguidi, known as Il Bertoja
Il sogno di Giacobbe
Studi per composizioni
(Giacobbe's dream. Studies for compositions)
(verso) 1569 ca.
ivory paper, pen, sepia; 324x280
source: Farnese collection
inventory: 931 (verso)

Perin del Vaga (attr.)
La deposizione
(The Entombment)
1540?
red-ochre Indian ink and white lead on
watercolour paper; mm 356x271
source: Firmian collection
inventory: 96

204

Tintoretto
Studio per la 'Battaglia sul Taro'
Study for the «Battle on the Taro»
1578 ca.
oil, tempera, black pen, mm 242x380
source: Bourbon collection
inventory: 1031

Guido Reni
Studio di figura ammantata
(Study of a cloaked figure) 1617-18
black pencil and white lead relief;
mm 426x239
source: Bourbon collection, inv. 702
It is the preparatory study for the figure of
Our Lady of Sorrows in the painting of the
Crocifissione (Crucifixion), done for the
church of the Cappuccini in Bologna,
presumably in 1617-18 and now kept in
the picture gallery of that city.

Jusepe de Ribera
Testa maschile grottesca
(Grotesque male head)
1622 ca.
red-ochre on white paper
mm 225x185
source: Firmian collection
inventory: 705
The accurate and clear-cut stroke of the

red-ochre and the hatching at parallel
and crossed intervals are common
characteristics in the early works of the
artist using the same technique. The
study is a preparation for the engraving
to which it corresponds precisely. Other
drawings are related to this for the
theme and technique used.

Jacques Callot
Studio per progetto da tavola o
progetto di fontana
(Study for table decoration or
for a fountain)
1615-17
red-ochre on white paper, filigree,
mm 401x282
source: Bourbon collection
inventory: 1002

208

Aniello Falcone
Testa di guerriero e studio di elmo
(Head of a soldier and study of a helmet)
1640 ca.
red-ochre on white paper mm 480x255
source: Bourbon collection
inventory: 125

It is one of the best examples of Falcone's graphic production for the extreme refinement of its pictorial stroke, calling to mind suggestions of the Roman production of Sacchi and Poussin. This style remains typical in the drawing of the master from then on (1640 ca.).

Massimo Stanzione
Suonatore di tromba
(Trumpeter)
1640 ca.
charcoal on greenish paper,
mm 308x245
source: Bourbon collection
inventory: 1054

210

Rembrandt Harmenszoon van Rijn
Giuditta decapita Oloferne
(Judith beheads Holofernes)
1650-55
pen and bistre, light brown paper
mm 182x150
source: Firmian collection
inventory: 1004
It is to be considered one of the most

successful results of the graphic
production of the artist around the years
1650-55.
In the collection it goes together with
another sheet of *Giuseppe che spiega i
sogni al Faraone* (Giuseppe explaining
his dreams to the Pharaoh), now
considered a production of the
Workshop.

52

Bernardo Cavallino
Studi di nudo virile
(Study of a virile nude)
1635-40
Red-ochre on ivory paper;
mm 209x211
source: Firmian collection
inventory: 139

Mattia Preti
*Studi per la cupola di San Biagio
a Modena*
(Study for the Dome of San Biagio
at Modena)
1653-56
charcoal, red-ochre, red and grey
watercolour on ivory paper
mm 410x276
source: Bourbon collection
inventory: 140

212

Luca Giordano
Il sacrificio di Manoah
(The Sacrifice by Manoah)
1656-60
pen, strokes of red-ochre on white paper
mm 241x321
source: Bourbon collection
inventory: 985

Gaspar van Wittel
*Veduta del monastero
di Grottaminarda*
(View of the monastery
of Grottaminarda)
1700 ca.
pencil, pen, ink and watercolour
on white paper;
mm 285x423
source: Astarita collection
inventory: 1753

214

Francesco Solimena
Studio per volto di giovane
(Study of young man's face), 1728
red-ochre on white paper
mm 178x180
source: Firmian collection
inventory: 1635
It is the study of the face of the young
page boy who appears on the left in the
painting of the *Conte Althann presenta
l'inventario della pinacoteca
imperiale all'imperatore Carlo VI
d'Asburgo* (Count Althann shows the
inventory of the Imperial Picture Gallery
to the emperor Charles VI of Hapsburg),
painted by Solimena in 1728 and kept
in Vienna, in the Kunsthistorisches
Museum.

Giacinto Gigante
Santa Maria Donnaregina
signed and dated 1865
pencil, pen and ink, watercolour;
mm 422x331; squared
source: Astarita collection
inventory: 5209

The watercolour belongs to a series of
sketches, taken from the convent of
Santa Maria Donnaregina in Naples,
perhaps commissioned by the abbess. It
is the last period of Gigante's
production, maybe the most intimate
and inclined to a new kind of sensitivity.

Albrecht Dürer
La passeggiata
(The walk), 1496-1498
burin; mm 195x120
source: Firmian collection
inventory: I.G.M.N. 89024
It represents the old theme of the
Vanitas Vanitatum: the young lovers
are walking in a pleasant spot, but
death is spying on them, unseen, behind
a tree. Datable to the early period of the
artist, between 1496 and 1498.

216

Annibale Carracci
Sileno ebbro (La tazza Farnese)
(Drunken Silenus - Farnese cup)
1597-1600
burin on silver;
diameter mm 323
source: Farnese collection
inventory: 801
Made for Cardinal Odoardo Farnese, it was described as a silver 'saucer' in the inventory of the Palazzo del Giardino of Parma in 1708. Many are the drawings which document the study of the work, surely inspired by the past. According to Bellori, Agostino Carracci also produced a similar work for Cardinal Farnese, confirmed by the survival of some drawings.

218

The Decorative Arts

The decorative art collections of the Museum of Capodimonte include an exceptional number of works belonging to the most diverse fields of artistic production: ivories, ambers, enamels, small bronzes, jewellery, carved rock crystals, medals and small plates, semi-precious stones, curiosities from *Wunderkammer*, weapons, tapestries, potteries, glass, silvers, shepherd figures, ceroplastics, clocks, jewels, furniture and other various and refined fittings. The Farnese Collection is the original part of the Capodimonte collection. It includes sculptures and items of minor arts among which the Farnese *Cofanetto* (Casket) stands out, sole existing example of 16th century jewellery, made of gilded silver and rock crystal, and used to keep Alessandro Farnese's bibliographic rare items. This collection, which marks the beginning of the museum was enlarged by the Bourbons, and increased through the years with the acquisition of collections of remarkable interest. The most important are the purchase of the Borgiano Museum in Velletri, by Ferdinand I in 1817; the donation of Alfonso d'Avalos, the marquis del Vasto and the Prince of Pescara in 1862; and, more recently in 1958, the gift of the precious collection of about 1,300 pieces gathered together by the 'commendatore' Mario De Ciccio, to mention only the most important ones. De Ciccio was one of the most famous Italian collectors of the first half of this century and his gifts considerably increased the department of decorative arts of the museum.

The most substantial group of items is undoubtedly the Royal Collection of weapons, which has about 4,000 pieces, one of the most important collections of its kind. It includes a more antique group made up of the Farnese family armoury, which goes back to the end of the 16th century-beginning of the 17th century, a rich collection of refined and valuable German and Northern Italian weapons, and a Bourbon collection of the 18th-19th centuries. This group was specifically collected by the kings of Naples, and included the production of the Royal Factory of Naples, founded by king Charles in 1734, after he ascended the throne of the Two Sicilies. Furthermore, there are the series of Madrilenian items brought to Naples by Charles of Bourbon, as well as rifles and guns of English manufacture, and some Eastern weapons, from the Borgia collection.

The pottery collection, made up of more than 4,000 items of majolicas, chinas and potteries, is exceptionally rich. The majolica department, mainly from the De Ciccio Collection, includes Hispano-Arab majolicas of the 15th-16th centuries, produced in Manises (Valenza); Persian and Syrian majolicas of the 13th and 14th centuries; and Italian majolicas, from the 16th to the 18th centuries, produced in Faenza, Florence, Venice, Siena, Urbino, Casteldurante, Deruta, Gubbio, Cafaggiolo, Orvieto, Naples, Savona, Mantua, Milan, Bologna and Castelli.

The porcelain collection includes items from the factory of Capodimonte, famous producer of soft paste porcelain, founded by Charles of Bourbon. It operated from 1743 to 1759 and its statuettes, groups and sets of great value have been kept together with the *Gabinetto di porcellana* (Porcelain Room), made for the Royal Palace of Portici, then dismantled and transferred to Capodimonte in 1864. Besides some Carolingian porcelain, the museum can boast a conspicuous collection of porcelains and biscuit from the Royal Factory of Naples, founded by Ferdinand in 1771, after the transfer of the factory of Capodimonte to Spain. Other types of porcelain housed in the museum are French porcelains of the first decades of the 19th century, decorated in Naples with illustrations of the costumes of the period, Neapolitan sights, and other motifs of neo-classical taste, and porcelain produced in Ginori di Doccia, Vinovo, Venezia and other Italian factories.

Many are the foreign producers represented and they are among the most famous and well known in Europe in the 18th century. We can find not only objects from Meissen, but also Sèvres, Wedgwood, Berlin, Vienna, Ludwigsburg, Frankenthal (Carlo Teodoro epoch, 1762-1798), Hochst, Zurigo, Derby-Chelsea (England). The section is completed by a fairly large collection of porcelains from the Far East made in the Chinese factories of Kangxi (1662- 1722) and Qianlong (1736- 1795), objects produced by the Indian Company and Japanese porcelains of the 18th century.

The group of potteries includes important 19th century pieces from Giustiniani's and Del Vecchio's factories, to which refined examples of the Palermitan factories of Malvica are to be added.

The textile collection of the museum includes a large number of tapestries and a scant collection of embroideries, laces and fabrics. The tapestries with the episodes of the *Battaglia di Pavia* (Battle of Pavia) and Flemish masterpieces of the 16th century donated by d'Avalos stand out together with some valuable Florentine examples of the same century.

Furthermore, the museum houses a precious example of the series of twelve tapestries *Storie di Don Chisciotte* (Stories of Don Quixote) of French Gobelins origin (donated in 1745 by Louis XV to the Prince of Campofiorito and given by the latter to Charles of Bourbon to decorate the Royal Palace of Caserta), and innumerable examples produced by the Royal Factory of Tapestries founded by Charles of Bourbon in Naples in 1737, and continued by Ferdinard IV to fulfil the need to decorate and furnish the vast wall spaces of the various royal palaces.

Two more groups are also worthy of note, the precious collection of Gothic ivories and enamels, mainly coming from the Museum Borgiano of Velletri, and a fairly substantial collection of items produced with precious and rare materials (amber, deer and rhinoceros horn, coconuts mounted on metal, ostrich eggs, semi-precious stones, carved crystal rocks). These constitute an interesting collection of curiosities worthy of the most famous 'rooms of wonder' of the 16th and 17th centuries. Of special relevance are the collections of Renaissance and Manneristic small bronzes also because they contain works of famous artists, among whom are Gianbologna, Guglielmo Della Porta and Francesco di Giorgio Martini. Of no less importance are the collection of Renaissance medals and small plates, and a conspicuous collection of Islamic art, which includes the rare *Globo Celeste* (Celestial Globe) of 1225, and two planisferic astrolabes, works of extreme rarity, probably going back to the end of the 13th century and the beginning of the 14th.

The merit of having acquired the precious collection of glass now in Capodimonte is to be attributed to the collectionist Mario De Ciccio. These objects are made of high quality and rare glass, mainly of Venetian production, or else they belong to that not always clearly definable group called 'façon de Venice'. The epoch extends from the end of the 15th century to the 16th and from the 17th to the end of the 18th. All the techniques used in Murano in those days are represented here, from the so-called 'crystalline', to the enamelware, the white 'milk-scab', the 'chalcedony', the filigree or reticello, the glass 'a penne', down to 'frosted' glass.

The furniture and furnishing objects of the Historical Apartment date back to the period from the second half of the 18th century to the end of the 19th. No Carolingean items are present in the collection but, on the other hand, the collection includes precious masterpieces of the cabinet making of the epoch of Ferdinand IV and Maria Carolina. These came from Royal residences, among which are the Villa Favorita of Resina and the Real Sito di Carditello. Worthy of note are also the precious furniture of the Joachim Murat period, coming directly from Napoleonic residences, and some curious Neapolitan furniture. Among these are the most original items of 19th century Neapolitan art, made precious with various materials, such as lava from Vesuvius, porcelain, semi-precious stones and bronzes, datable to the Bourbon restoration.

Paris
*Trittico con Madonna con Bambino,
Incoronazione della Vergine e altre
scene*
(Tryptich of Madonna with Child,
Incoronation of the Virgin and other
scenes), 1290 ca.
ivory; h. cm 19; base cm 14
source: purchased Cardinal Ruffo, 1845
inventory: 10108 A.M.

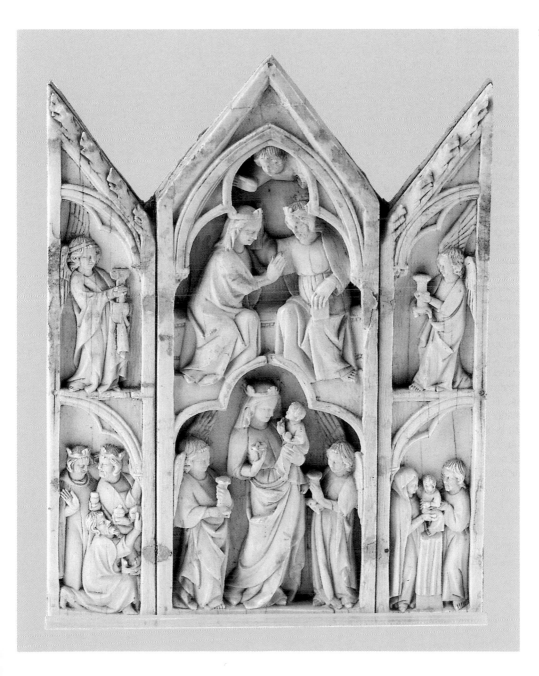

Indian Art (?)
Ventaglio
(Fan)
17th century
ivory; h. cm 54; diam. 26
source: Farnese collection
inventory: 10398 A.M.

Valle del Reno
Adorazione dei Magi
(Adoration of the Magi)
end of the 13th century
glaze (champlevé) on copper;
h. cm 14; base cm 10
source: Borgia collection
inventory: 10417 Λ.M.

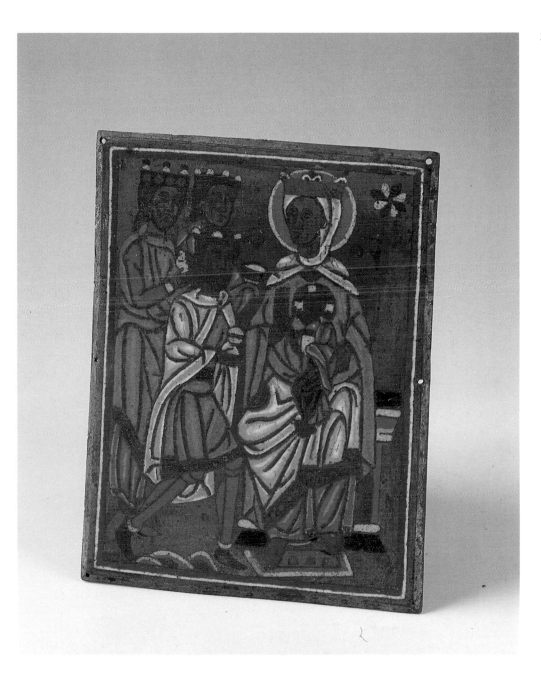

Limoges
Riccio di Pastorale
(Hook of Pastoral Crook)
4th decade of the 13th century
embossed, carved, gilded and glazed
(champlevé) fused copper;
h. cm 34.4 diam. hook 12.2
source: Borgia Collection
inventory: 10420 A.M.
Splendid example of the Limoges

goldsmiths' art which, since the end of
the 7th decade of the 12th century, had
become the most important western
centre of production of glazed copper
sacred vestments.
In the hook, Saint Michael the
Archangel killing the dragon, is
represented. Other examples of this can
be found in Italian and foreign
museums.

Nicolò Lionello
Pace
('Peace', a liturgical object)
1440-1450 ca.
Gilded silver and glaze;
h. cm 21.5x14.5
source: Borgia collection
inventory: 10418 A.M.

France

Cartagloria
(Altar-card)
first half of the 16th century
Embroidered cloth and enamels;
h. cm 40; width cm 105
source: Borgia collection
inventory: 10322 A.M.
It comes from the Monastery of

Fontevrault and became part of the
Borgia collection after 1799. It is made
up of three panels of white silk
embroidered with golden and silk
threads. In the central panel there are
three enamels, the *Natività di Cristo*
(Nativity of Christ), the *Crocifissione*
(Crucifixion), and the *Noli me tangere*,
presumably added to the altar-card later.

Nottingham or York
Polittico con la Crocifissione e sei scene della Passione di Cristo
(Polyptych with the Crucifixion and six scenes of the Passion of Christ)
(detail in the photo)
middle of the 15th century
alabaster, glasses 'eglomisés'; h. cm 162
width cm 360
source: Naples, Sacristy of the church of San Giovanni a Carbonara, 1809
inventory: 10816 A.M.
The seven alabaster high-reliefs represent: in the centre the *Crocifissione* (Crucifixion); on the left, *il Bacio di Giuda,* (the Kiss of Judas), *l'Arresto di Gesù (*the Arrest of Jesus), *l'Andata al Calvario* (The path to Calvary); on the right, *la Discesa dalla Croce* (Taking down from the Cross), *la Deposizione* (The Entombment), *la Resurrezione* (the Resurrection). It is not the only example of this kind of art work to reach Italy, but it stands out for its quality, the complexity of the scene and its state of conservation. It retains, in fact, ample traces of the old polychrome, of the framing in pierced pinnacles, and vast surviving areas of the eglomisés glasses which once embellished the work.

Antonio Carracci
*Madonna col Bambino e San
Francesco
Annunciazione*
(Madonna with Child and Saint Francis
- The Annunciation)
painted alabaster;
h. cm 22; width cm 18
source: Farnese collection
inventory: 930 Q

230

Syria or Egypt
Globo Celeste
(Celestial Globe)
dated 1225
cast bronze encrusted in silver and
copper; diam. 22.1
source: Borgia collection
inventory: 112091
This object, one of the oldest celestial
globes, was commissioned for the sultan
Ayyubide Al Kamil (1218-1237) in 1225.
The globe is made up of two
hemispheres on which are engraved the
drawings of the forty-eight
constellations visible in the celestial
vault, according to the standards
already decided by Ptolemy. The names
of the most important stars are written
in full, whereas all the others are
identified with the corresponding
number of the treatise on fixed stars by
Al-Sufi. There are two 13th century
celestial globes kept respectively in the
British Museum and in the Louvre.

Produced in Milan

Gioco di rotella e caschetto all'eroica di Alessandro Farnese
(Round shield and small helmet belonged to Alessandro Farnese)
1560 ca.
Blued, damascened, gilt, enamelled iron; h. cm 29, width cm 32, depth 13
source: Farnese collection
inventory: 3737, 3738 O.A

Presumably belonging to the time of the marriage of Alessandro Farnese with Maria of Portugal (1565), they include episodes from Roman history.
On the round shield is the episode of Horatius Cocles who defends the bridge on the Tiber, on the small helmet the representation of Martius Curtius and the justice of Trajan. The two objects, among the best works of the famous Milanese factory of the second half of the century, decidedly belong to the group of the four sets of the 'bourguignotte' (type of helmet) and round shield attributed to the 'master of 1563', as it appears from the date on the round shield marked 'BPF'. The same abbreviation was also found in the Rothschild collection.

Spain, 15th century
Coppia di astrolabi
(Pair of astrolabes)
1476 ca.
Brass; diam. 17.9x18.1
source: Borgia collection
inventory: 112098 and 112099 A.M.

234

The Royal Steel Factory
Daga da caccia
(Hunting dagger)
end of the 18th century
Smooth steel blade, handle, hilt and
sheath with ornaments and medallions
of polished steel, sheath made of white
shagreen h. cm 70
source: Royal Bourbon Collections

inventory: 2837 OA
It is to date one of the rare identified
works of the Royal Steel Factory,
founded about 1782, to which craftsmen
were called purposely from Vienna.
It was part of the Royal Porcelain
Factory and both factories were under
the management of Domenico Venuti.

Pisanello
Medal of Lionello d'Este, 1444
melted bronze; cm 101
source: Farnese collection, inv.: 67522
On the front it represents the bust of
Lionello d'Este and on the back, a lion
stopped by an amoretto holding a musical
score. In the background is a rock and a
shrub on which a dove is perching. Made
in 1444 in Ferrara for the marriage of
Lionello with Maria d'Aragona.

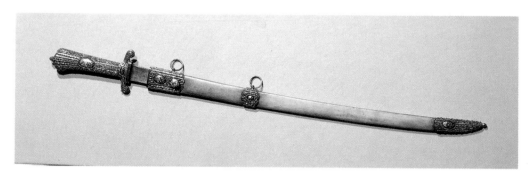

**Manno di Bastiano Sbarri and
Giovanni Desiderio Bernardi**
Cofanetto Farnese
(Farnese Casket), 1548-1561
Golden silver, crystal rock, enamel, lapis
lazuli; h. cm 49
source: Farnese collection
inventory: 10507 A.M.
Masterpiece of jewellery in the
Mannerist style, created for the cardinal
Alessandro Farnese. The casket, made to
keep manuscripts and precious books, is
decorated with embossed reliefs on all
sides, internally, externally and
underneath. Four divinities are put in
the corners and on the top. At the centre
of the lid is the image of Hercules. The
six crystal rock ovals, placed two by two
on the long sides and one on each of the
short sides, represent the Battle of the
Amazons and the Battle of the Centaurs
on the front, a naval battle on the left,
the Hunt of the Calidonian wild boar
and the Triumph of Bacchus on the
back, and finally the Race of the
quadrigae (two-wheeled chariots drawn
by four horses) in the circus on the
right.

Giovanni Desiderio Bernardi
Augusto e la Sibilla?
(Augustus and the Sibyl?)
1535 ca.
Crystal rock; h. cm 10.6;
Width cm 85
source: Farnese collection
inventory: 10289 A.M.

238

Jacob Miller the Elder
Diana cacciatrice sul cervo
(Diana, the huntress, on a deer)
Table trophy
gilded silver; h. cm 31.5
source: Farnese collection
inventory: 10508 A.M.
This peculiar object is a precious table trophy, provided with a mechanism contained in the octagonal base which makes it move. The head of the deer, that can be dismantled, serves as a lid and as a goblet. It bears the initials I.M. which are related to the goldsmith Jacob Miller the Elder from Augusta. This type of object was typical of the refined European centres of the late mannerist culture and we know of several examples done by different artists, all working in the famous German centre between the last decades of the 16th century and the early decades of the 17th century.

Guido Mazzoni
Busto di Alfonso Duca di Calabria
(Bust of Alfonso Duke of Calabria)
1492-1493 ca.
h. cm 42
source: Naples, church of Santa Maria
di Monteoliveto
inventory: 10527 A.M
For a long time thought to be a portrait
of Alfonso I, King of Naples, this bronze
bust is now unanimously considered as
a portrait of Alfonso II. The attribution
to Mazzoni is generally accepted.
The work has been made with the
highly realistic and refined style typical
Mazzoni's terracotta works.
When the same style is adopted for
works made of bronze, they acquire an
antique character which makes them
similar to Roman busts.

Guglielmo della Porta
Paolo III Farnese
(Paul III Farnese)
· 1546
marble; h. cm 95
source: Farnese collection
inventory: 10514 A.M.
The bust is unanimously identified with
the sculpture of the Pope which Della

Porta made in 1546 for a hall in the
Farnese Palace in Rome. The sculptor
used two different types of marble for the
rich cope. On the edges of the mantle, the
allegories of *Abbondanza* (Abundance),
Pace (Peace) and *Vittoria* (Victory) are
recognisable. The drapery is pinned with
a rare jewel, of refined 15 th century
origin.

Francesco di Giorgio Martini
David
1475-1485
Bronze; h. cm 33
source: Farnese collection
inventory: 10534 A.M.
This bronze is surprising for its unusual
iconography which combines the
medieval tradition representing David as
a bearded old prophet, with the
Renaissance tradition representing him
as the victorious young hero over
Goliath, an innovation introduced for
the first time in sculpture by Donatello.
The attribution to Francesco Martini is
generally accepted.

Next page
Giambologna
Mercurio
(Mercury)
Bronze; h. cm 58.4
source: Farnese collection
inventory: 10784 A.M.
This bronze is mentioned in a letter of
13th June 1579, sent by Giambologna to
Ottavio Farnese, Archduke of Parma, in
which the sculptor refers to having
already delivered this work. At present
there are no elements to date it more
precisely. The work represents a reduced
edition, with variations, of the big
bronze in the National Museum of
Florence, cast in 1564.

Giambologna
Ercole e il cinghiale di Erimanto
(Hercules and the wild boar of
Erimanto)
Bronze; h. cm 44
source: Farnese collection
inventory: 10785 A.M.
It represents the fourth labour of
Hercules and reproduces one of the six
silver subjects of the Uffizi gallery. The
wax mould for the castings was,
perhaps, prepared by Antonio Fusini, in
1587. With a silver version of *Ercole che
sostiene i cieli* (Hercules supporting the
skies), it was moulded by Iacopo Bylvet.

242

Guglielmo della Porta
Ercole fanciullo che strozza i serpenti
(Hercules as a child strangling the
snakes), before 1575
bronze; h. cm 96
source: Farnese collection
inventory: 10520 A.M.
It comes from the Farnese Palace in Rome
and belongs to a group of works sold in
1575 by della Porta himself to the Duke of
Parma, Ottavio Farnese. The old
inventories mention two similar examples.

Giambologna
Ratto di una sabina
(Rape of a Sabine), 1579
Bronze; h. cm 98.1
source: Farnese collection
inventory: 10524 AM
This bronze group, made by
Giambologna for the Archduke of
Parma in June 1579, represents the
prototype of the great marble group,
exhibited in 1583, in the Loggia dei
Lanzi in Florence.

Produced in Flanders, 16th century

Cattura di Francesco I
(Capture of King Francis I of France),
1530 ca.
Wool, silk, gold; h. cm 435, width
cm 880
source: d'Avalos donation inv.: 144489
It belongs to a series of seven tapestries
illustrating the main episodes of the famous Battle of Pavia (1525), during which the army of Don Ferrante d'Avalos, marquis of Pescara, won and captured King Francis I of France. These tapestries were woven on cartoons (now kept in the Louvre) by Bernard Van Orley in Brussels soon after these events and were then given to Charles V in 1531, by some merchants of Brussels. For several years they decorated the Imperial Palace of Brussels. It is unknown how they came into d'Avalos's possession, but it is clear that they must have belonged to the descendants of the marquis of Pescara, who played a major role in the battle.

247

Florence, Plant of semi-precious
stones
Cassetta (Small case)
second half of the 17th century
Bas relief with semi-precious stones,
ebony, gilded copper;
h. cm 19, width cm 42
source: Farnese collection
inventory: 10185

248

**Royal Factory of Tapestries of Naples
Pietro Duranti**
*Don Chisciotte fa chiedere alla
duchessa il permesso di vederla*
(A man asks the Duchess on behalf of
Don Quixote for permission to see her)
1771 ca.
wool, silk; h. cm 378x337
source: Royal Bourbon collections
inventory: 7255 O.A.

It belongs to the series of tapestries with
Stories of Don Quixote, woven by Pietro
Duranti to complete the twelve tapestries,
produced in the atelier Jans and Lefebvre
of the factory of Gobelins between 1730
and 1733. This series was donated by
Louis XV to the Duke of Campofiorito,
ambassador of Spain in Paris, and given
by him to Charles of Bourbon, to
decorate the Palace of Caserta.

.

Urbino, factory of Orazio Fontana
Rinfrescatoio
(Cooler), 1560-1570
Majolica covered with glass; h. cm 32
diam. 53
source: M. De Ciccio donation, 1958
inventory: 240
It was commissioned by the Duke

Guidobaldo II della Rovere to the
factory of Orazio Fontana, between 1560
and 1570 ca. It is completely covered
with a kind of grotesque decoration, very
popular in the 16th century. The inside
of the cooler is painted entirely with a
Roman scene, probably based on an
engraving.

Meissen
Boccale da birra a cineserie
(Beer tankard with chinoiseries)
1730-1740
Painted and gilded china; gilded silver;
h. cm 23; diam. 11
source: M. De Ciccio, 1958
inventory: 441253

Meissen
Dama con cagnolino
(Lady with small dog)
middle of the 18th century
Polychrome porcelain; h. cm 28
source: M. De Ciccio, 1958
inventory: 263

Royal Factory of Capodimonte
Specchiera
(Large Mirror)
1750-1755
Painted and enamelled porcelain;
h. cm 125, b. cm 71
source: Royal Bourbon collections
inventory: 6233 O.A.

Royal Factory of Capodimonte
Gabinetto di porcellana del Palazzo di Portici 1757-1759
(Porcelain private room of the Palace of Portici)
Painted and enamelled porcelain, stucco work;
cm 6.75x4.80x5.13
source: Royal Palace of Portici;

Royal Bourbon Collections
inventory: 1382 O.A.
Probably planned as a private parlour of Queen Maria Amalia, it represents the highest artistic expression of the Royal Factory of Capodimonte. The direction of the work, planned by the scenographer Giovan Battista Natali, was entrusted to Giuseppe Gricci helped,

for the painted decoration, by Sigmund Fischer and Luigi Restile.
It is made up of porcelain slabs, fixed with screws to a supporting wooden wall and decorated with festoons, musical trophies, cartouches and scenes illustrated with 'chinoiseries', based on the French models of Watteau and Boucher.

Royal Factory of Capodimonte
Vaso biansato
(Two-handled vase)
1745-1750
Painted and enamelled porcelain;
h. cm 23
source: M. De Ciccio donation, 1958
inventory: 320

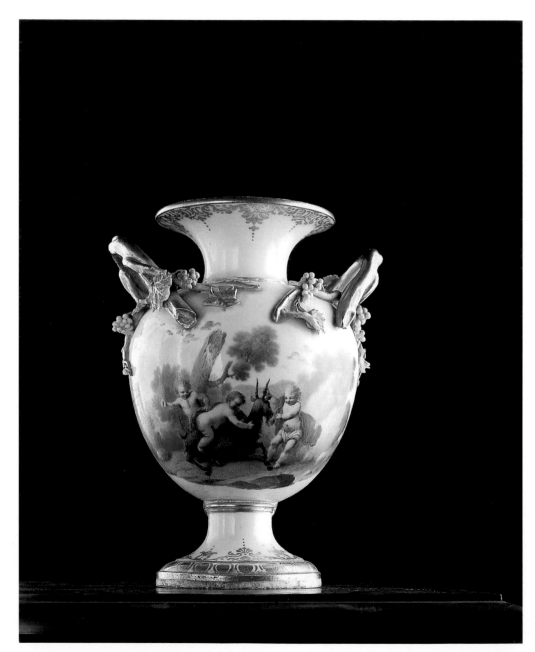

Royal Factory of Capodimonte
Bacile a conchiglia
(Basin in the shape of a shell)
1745 ca.
White porcelain; h. cm 13; b. 33
source: Royal Bourbon collections
inventory: 6232 O.A.

Royal Factory of Capodimonte
Giuseppe Gricci
Immacolata Concezione
(Immaculate Conception), 1744-1745 ca.
White porcelain
Marked: Giglio Azzurro (Light Blue lily)
h. cm 35
source: purchased Alfonso Jodice, 1972
inventory: 7817 O.A.
The existence of a 'Conception' is
mentioned among the works done by

Giuseppe Gricci, head-modeller of the
Royal Factory, between December 1744
and August 1745. The small but
numerous imperfections which can be
seen in the cob are typical of the
production of the early years, due to the
not yet perfected technical procedures.
The iconographic model might have
been taken from the silver works in
relief made in Neapolitan factories in
the 17th and 18th centuries.

Royal Factory of Capodimonte
Giuseppe Gricci
Crocifisso
(Crucifix) 1745 ca.
White porcelain; h. cm 89
Marked: Giglio Azzurro (Light blue lily)
source: Royal Bourbon Collections
inventory: 5233 O.A.
It is part of a set of liturgical tools
including also six candlesticks,
produced for the private chapel of the
Royal Palace of Portici.

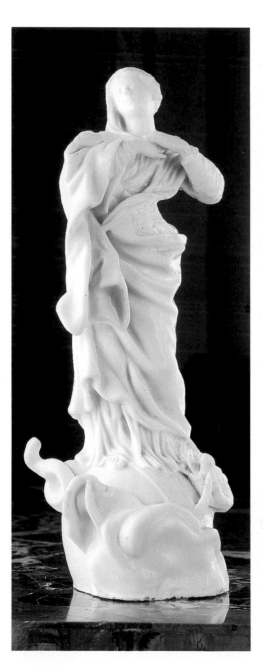

Royal Factory of Capodimonte
Venditore di taralli
(Seller of taralli - A kind of pastry)
1750-1752
Painted and enamelled porcelain;
h. cm 17
source: M. De Ciccio donation, 1958
inventory: 330

Royal Factory of Capodimonte
La Scuola di Ricamo
(The embroidery school)
1750 ca.
Painted and gilded porcelain;
h. cm 14.2
source: M. De Ciccio donation, 1958
inventory: 377

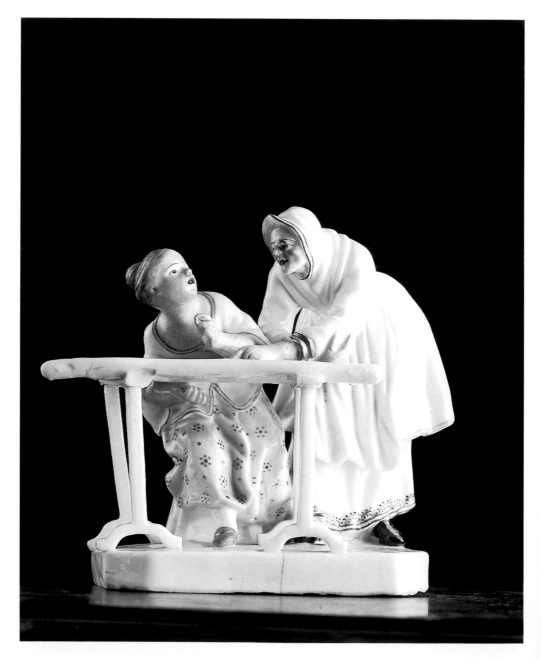

Royal Porcelain Factory of Naples
*Déjeuneur (tazze, piattino,
zuccheriera, lattiera, caffettiera,
vassoio)*
(Breakfast set: cups, saucer, sugar bowl,
milk jug, coffee-pot, tray)
Tray; cm 32x34
Painted, gilded and gilded in relief
porcelain
source: M. De Ciccio, 1958
inventory: 497

Royal Porcelain Factory of Naples
(1771-1806)
Déjeuner con scene 'Etrusche'
(Breakfast set with 'Etruscan' scenes)
Painted and gilded porcelain
Tray; cm 32.5
source: Royal Bourbon Collections
inventory: 5065 OA

Royal Porcelain Factory of Naples
Servizio dell'oca o delle vedute napoletane: Zuppiera ovale
(Dinner set called 'of the goose' or 'of the Neapolitan views': Oval tureen)
Polychrome and gilded porcelain
Marked: N with a blue crown;
h. cm 39.5
source: Royal Bourbon Collections
inventory: 5594 OA
This is a dinner set made for the royal family, and called after the 'putto' (a small boy) strangling a goose on top of the lid. The putto and the goose function as a knob. This kind of decoration, often found on soup tureens, is taken from a Hellenistic sculpture kept in the Capitolini Museums. The set counts over three hundred pieces of china and is decorated with views of the Royal Residences and of the most picturesque sights of Naples during the reign of the Bourbons. The images are based on prints of the time made by Neapolitan and foreign craftsmen.

Previous page
Royal Porcelain Factory of Naples
Filippo Tagliolini
Trionfo di Bacco e Sileno
(Triumph of Bacchus and Silenus)
Biscuit; h. cm 61
source: Royal Bourbon Collections
inventory: 1065
Made under the direction of Filippo
Tagliolini, head-modeller of the Royal
Factory, this work is made up of two

separate parts. The central group with
Silenus and Bacchus is based on a
classic prototype existing in the 18th
century in Villa Borghese. The basement
is made up of a dancing faun, a
Dionysian priest and a bacchante with a
panther. When creating porcelain
statues with more than one character,
the artist would introduce original
figures next to the ones based on
ancient models.

Royal Porcelain Factory of Naples
Filippo Tagliolini
Amore e Psiche
(Cupid and Psyche)
Biscuit; h. cm 5
source: Royal Bourbon Collections
inventory: 5205 O. A.

Royal Porcelain Factory of Naples
Filippo Tagliolini
Busto di Maria Carolina
(Bust of Maria Carolina)
Biscuit; h. cm 55
source: Royal Bourbon Collections
inventory:. 5338 O. A.

Royal Porcelain Factory of Naples
Filippo Tagliolini
L'Aurora
(Aurora)
1806 ca.
Biscuit, h. cm 37.5 (Dawn)
source: Royal Bourbon collections
inventory: 5116 O. A.
For the production of this imposing group
Tagliolini probably drew inspiration from
the more famous *Aurora* by Guido Reni
in the Palazzo Rospigliosi. In Reni's work
the cart is driven by Sun-Apollo, a figure
which was not introduced by Tagliolini.
The 'biga' (a two-horse chariot), inspired
by classic representations is surrounded by
twelve young women, the Hours, and
preceded by Aurora, sided by two putti
(small boys). One putto has a quiver and
bow and represents 'Amor Felice' while the
other, melancholic and with joined hands,
represents 'Amor Infelice'.

Royal Porcelain Factory of Naples
Gruppo Bernesco
(Bernese group)
second half of the 18th century
Polychrome porcelain, h. cm 21.5
source: M. De Ciccio donation, 1958
inventory: 1347

268

Royal Porcelain Factory of Naples
Orologio (Clock)
1796-1806
Painted and gilded porcelain, biscuit,
various types of marble and gilded
bronze, cm 116x67x46.5
source: Royal Bourbon Collections
inventory: 5113 O. A.
It belongs to a set of four clocks, produced
for the apartments in the Royal Palace of
Naples of the heir apparent, Francesco, on
the occasion of his wedding with M.

Clementina d'Austria in 1797. This fact
seems confirmed by the two initials 'FC',
that appear on the back of the pendulum
clock. The clock case, probably made in
Rome, is embellished with rare marbles
and gilt bronzes and is supported by four
telamones. At the top of the clock, two
figures, representing an allegory of war,
are surrounded by Egyptian canopic
vases. The vases were copied from a
famous model kept, since the 18th
century, in the Musei Capitolini.

Vienna
Due piatti con vedute di Napoli e Vienna
(Two plates with views of Naples and Vienna)
1800-1801
Painted and gilded porcelain;
diam. 21.4
source: Royal Bourbon Collections
inventory: 6888, 7061 O. A.

Murano
Coppa
(Goblet)
15th century
Glass with polychrome enamels,
h. cm 16.5
source: M. De Ciccio donation, 1958
inventory: 709

Sèvres
Vaso con miniatura di Napoleone I
(Vase with miniature of Napoleon I)
1810 ca.
Painted and gilded porcelain; h. cm 55
source: Royal Bourbon Collections
inventory: 6990 O. A.
The miniature is signed by 'Georgct'

Murano
Coppa con coperchio
(Goblet with lid)
16th century
Glass 'a reticello'; h. cm 23
source: M. De Ciccio donation, 1958
inventory: 620

Spain
Bicchiere da viaggio
(Travel glass)
17th century
Glass; h. cm 10, diam. base 6.5
source: M. De Ciccio donation, 1958
inventory: 642

Murano
Bottiglia
(Bottle)
18th century
Calcedonian glass; h. cm 30
source: M. De Ciccio donation, 1958
inventory: 649

France
Fiasca da pellegrino
(Pilgrim flask)
first half of the 17th century
glass h. cm 28.2; base diam. 12
source: M De Ciccio donation, 1958
inventory: 713

Gio. Francesco Pieri
Il maestro di scuola
(Schoolmaster),
signed G. F. P. 1760
coloured waxes on a board
h. cm 43.5, Width cm 34.5
source: Royal Bourbon Collections
inventory: 7287 O A

Jean Louvet
Due lire armoniche o ghironde
(Two harmonic lyres or barrel organs)
signed J. Louvet in Paris and dated
respectively 1764 and 1780
Different types of wood, ivory, bone,
mother of pearl, h. cm 70, width cm 30
(each)
source: Royal Bourbon Collections
inventory: 3772 and 3773 M

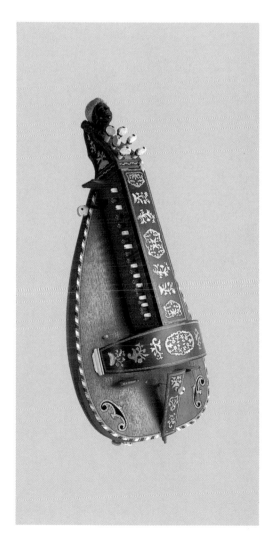
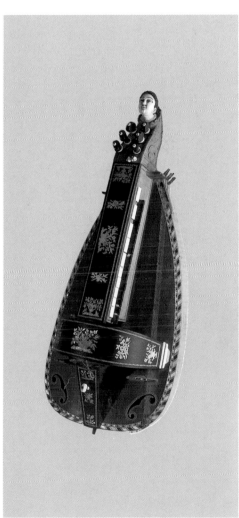

Neapolitan Factory
Gruppo Presepiale raffigurante
Natività con gloria d'Angeli
(Crib group representing Nativity with a Pride of Angels)
End of 18th century - beginning of 19th century
Wood, polychrome terracotta, glass, tow, iron and cork; total h. cm 100
source: E. and E. Catello donation, 1986
inventory: from 8516-8559 O.A.
This highly remarkable group of the

Nativity, with the Madonna, Saint Joseph and the Holy Child are the work of the sculptor Giuseppe Sanmartino. Salvatore Franco made the beautiful Angel in full relief, while other angels are attributed to equally famous artists specialised in the making of crib statuettes, such as Lorenzo Mosca, Nicola Ingaldo, Giuseppe Gori and Michele Trillocco. The animals are by Francesco Gallo and the Vassallo brothers.

Vienna
Cofano
(Casket)
1801 ca.
Mahogany, gilded bronze, biscuit,
eglomisè glass; h. cm 16; width cm 23;
depth. 13
source: Bourbon Royal Collections
inventory: 6819 OA

Joseph Martineau
Orologio
(Clock)
Veneered with walnut roots
Finishings in gilt bronze
cm 90x58x38
source: Royal Bourbon Collections
inventory: 2734 M.

Raffaello Rastelli
Orologio da tavolo con motivi egizi
(Table clock with Egyptian motifs)
On the back it bears the signature of
"Raffaello Rastelli Roma"
Aged red, porphyry, serpentine, basalt,
gilt bronze; h. cm 80; width cm 64.5;
depth 33
source: Royal Bourbon Collections
inventory: 3603 IM.

Royal craftsmen
Portantina
(Sedan chair)
1770 ca.
Carved, engraved wood varnished in light blue
cm 158x82x82
source: Royal Bourbon Collections
inventory: 3375 M.

Royal craftsmen
Tavolo parietale (Wall table)
First half of the 18th century
Carved, engraved, lacquered and gilt wood; top part veneered with black and aged white with alabaster edges.
cm 89x130x63
source: Royal Bourbon Collections
inventory: 2680 M.
It belongs to a pair of wall tables considered the highest example of Neapolitan baroque.

Domenico Vanotti
Tavola da gioco (Card table)
1796 ca.
Veneered and inlaid with exotic types of wood; cm 82x89x60; open 88.5
source: Royal Bourbon Collections
inventory: 2285 M.
It is veneered and inlaid with exotic types of wood with the symbols of love and music. It bears stylistic similarities with the works of Lumbard cabinet makers such as Giuseppe Maggiolini.

Naples-France
*Poltrona con veduta del Palazzo
dell'Eliseo a Parigi*
(Armchair with view of the Elysèe
Palace in Paris)
First decades of the 19th century
Painted and gilt wood, painted velvet;
h. cm 102; width cm 67; depth cm 49
source: Royal Bourbon Collections
inventory: 3476 IM.

284

Historical apartment
Salottino Pompeiano
(Pompeian parlour)
Third decade of the 19th century

**Royal Craftsmen (Nicola and Pietro
Fiore and Antonio Pittarelli?)**
*Sofa and two armchairs with dancing
maenads*
End of the 18th century
Carved, painted and gilt wood;
cm 95x175x55; cm 93x64x54

source: Royal Bourbon Collections
inventory: 4790, 4792, 4796 M.
In the middle there is a sofa with two
armchairs which belong to a set of four
sofas and eight armchairs that used to
decorate the walls of Villa Favorita in
Resina. The backs of this "suite", which
can be removed, are decorated with oval
panels portraying bacchantes, based on
Herculanensis models. The paintings
reflect the English taste of decorators
active in the circle of Robert Adam.

Martin-Guillaume Biennais
Tavolo da gioco
(Card table)
1802
Mahogany, gilt bronze; h. cm 58;
width cm 147
source: Royal Bourbon Collections
inventory: 1019 IM.
The original document of the sale of the
table to the general Joachim Murat is
still in the drawer.

Royal Factory of semi-precious
stones of Naples
Tavolo con scacchiera
(Table with chessboard)
first decades of the 18th century
Mosaic of semi-precious stones on
petrified wood, gilt bronze, marble;
h. cm 71; width cm 95
source: Royal Bourbon Collections
inventory: 3290 M.

Historical Apartment, Hall 81

Produced in Naples
Tavolo da centro (Centre table)
first decades of the 19th century
Various types of marble, antique marble,
gilt bronze, lava; cm 220x134
source: Royal Bourbon Collections
inventory: 3328 M.
The rim is decorated with lava
medallions on which are portraits of the
Kings of Naples.

Historical Apartment, Hall 80

Produced in Naples
Voliera, fioriera, acquario
(Aviary, flower pot holder, aquarium)
1800-1825 ca.
Mahogany, gilt bronze, crystal;
h. cm 250, diam. 200
source: Royal Bourbon Collections
inventory: 10153 M.
In the middle of the room, a peculiar piece of furniture made in a Neapolitan factory is decorated with magnificent bronze fittings suitable for three different uses. The lower part holds a fish tank. The table, on which is placed a birdcage, is used as a jardinière. Above that is the full relief rotating figure of Fortune, an adaptation in the Empire style of a Renaissance bronze by Denise Cattaneo.

Luigi Righetti
Tripode
(Tripod)
1815 ca.
Gilt and plated bronze, mosaic,
semi-precious stones;
h. cm 88, diam. 35
source: Royal Bourbon Collections
inventory: 1785 M.

Produced in Naples, 19th century
Giardiniera
(Jardinière)
1828
Mahogany, porcelain and gilt bronze
h. cm 137, diam. 130
source: Royal Bourbon Collections
inventory: 3732 M.

This jardinière is decorated with plates and porcelain vases bearing miniatures of the views of Naples, Pompeii, Royal Residences and the costumes of the time. It is a sort of monument to the tourist and folklore attractions of the Kingdom of Naples. A small picture is signed *Giovine* and dated 1828.

Produced in Naples
Tavolino
(Small table)
before 1829
Carved, engraved, painted and gilt
mahogany; watercolour on paper;
h. cm 82; top cm 74x49.5
source: Royal Bourbon Collections
inventory: 4047 M.

Produced in Naples, 19th century
Tavolino
(Small table)
1830-1832
Mahogany, bronze, gilt bronze; painted porcelain, marble, semi-precious stones.
cm 86x66
source: Royal Bourbon Collections
inventory: 4096 M.

The table has an extremely sophisticated top made of green Sicilian marble with marquetries and plant decorations made of marble in contrasting colours. There are twenty-five holes in which are inserted revolving medallions with a mechanism that starts a musical box. The outer medallions have on one-side twelve views of the royal sites, and on the other the names of the various members of the royal family. The inner medallions bear, on one side, the Bourbon crowned lily and the date 1830, and on the other, the picture of Francesco I.

The Villa of the Princes in the Park
of Capodimonte

The Park of Capodimonte

The Park of Capodimonte stretches over an area of about 124 hectares. Its trees are of extraordinary interest with more than 400 registered varieties including secular holm-oaks, oaks, lindens, cypresses, chestnuts, pines.

In 1735 Charles of Bourbon wanted it mainly for the hunting activity of himself and his court. After the completion of the preliminary procedures of purchases and expropriations from private citizens, Ferdinando Sanfelice drew up a plan trying to create a kind of harmony among the multitude of pre-existing structures. As a result, its structure is complex and sometimes contradictory, for the most covered by woods with different types of tree. At the entrance, it is shaped geometrically with five wide avenues leading off fan-wise from a vast elliptical space. On the other hand, the area situated on the borders and characterised by continuous variations in height, presents an irregular, spontaneous intertwining of the vegetation.

A series of buildings originally planned to hold the happenings of court life (Casina della Regina, Palazzina dei Principi), or to use as seats of royal factories (Edificio della Manifattura della Porcellana) are scattered throughout the wood. Others were used for religious purposes (Chiesa di San Gennaro, Eremo dei Cappuccini), others again, reserved to agricultural and zootechnic activities (Pheasantry, Cellar, Cowshed).

The historical cartography of the 18th century shows that there were some orchards and fenced gardens annexed to these buildings. However, they became part of the overall plan but were never fully incorporated into it so they formed a kind of addition. During the repeated changes, which took place in the first half of the 19th century and which modified the structure of the park exalting the landscape, a lot of the agricultural lands were eliminated, following the changing fashions. The only testimony to the pre-existing productivity is the Torre garden, situated at the extreme limits of the park, overlooking the slopes of the deep valley of San Rocco and bordering the lands of the convent of Santa Maria ai Monti. The place still retains the old Bourbon citrus orchard, although modified in the original structural plan. Beyond it is the secret garden, surrounded by walls, which originally kept rare ornamental species and exotic-fruit trees, such as pineapples (the 'heating systems' of which are mentioned in the archive documents and in the cartographic sources).

Another significant feature of the park is the 'English garden' belonging to the Casino dei Principi and annexed to the Capodimonte site during the Murat period, when the wood and the Royal Palace, until then separated by a public road, were united. All the open space surrounding the palace was better arranged and admission gates were provided to close off the entrance. Around the 1830's, the curving surface extending behind the Palazzina dei Principi was transformed with relation to the view of the sea and Vesuvius, according to the prevailing taste for landscapes, under the direction of the botanist Federico Denhardt, who experimented with rare, exotic cultivations such as the eucalyptus and the thuja. The Palazzina dei Principi was the old Casina dei marchesi di Acquaviva adapted according to the wishes of Francesco I as lodging for the children of the king.

After the Unification, Capodimonte became the seat of the Royal House of Savoy. Some changes were made mostly in the area next to the Royal Palace where different varieties of palms were planted, according to the 'orientalist' tendencies in fashion at the end of the 19th century. A brief mention should be made of the statues which in the past, as mentioned in the archives and the guide-books, were a notable presence in the park, ornamenting fountains, paths, avenues and shooting lodges. Unfortunately the only sculptures still surviving are those representing the twelve months, and the imposing statue of the Giant or of Hercules. The former group, the gift of Carthusian monks to Ferdinand IV in 1762, is by now almost all mutilated and headless and placed in niches of green in the elliptic space at the entrance. The statue of the Giant, made of antique fragments coming from the Farnese collections was once strategically placed at the end of the central avenues to create a visual impression.

The area of the park of Capodimonte in front of the Museum, arranged as a landscape garden.

The late 19th century layout of the so called 'view': the terrace, decorated with some varieties of palms, overlooks the city.

Bibliography

1824-1857
Real Museo Borbonico, 16 voll., Napoli 1824-1857.
1827
Guida del Real Museo Borbonico, Napoli 1827.
1866
Salazar, D., *Sul riordinamento della Pinacoteca del Museo Nazionale*, Napoli 1866.
1873
Fiorelli, G., *Del Museo Nazionale di Napoli*, Napoli 1873.
1874
Monaco, D., *Guida generale del Museo Nazionale di Napoli*, Napoli 1874.
1876
Alberti, A., *Guida illustrativa del Real Museo di Capodimonte*, Napoli 1876.
Migliozzi, A., *Nuova guida generale del Museo Nazionale di Napoli*, Napoli 1876.
1884
Sacco, A., *R. Museo di Capodimonte*, Napoli 1884.
1895
Faraglia, N.A., *La R. Pinacoteca di Napoli nel 1802*, in «Napoli Nobilissima» IV (1895), 109-111, 156-157.
Frizzoni, G., *La Pinacoteca del Museo Nazionale di Napoli nuovamente illustrata*, in «Napoli Nobilissima» IV (1895), 20-25.
Spinazzola, V., *La R. Pinacoteca del Museo Nazionale di Napoli. Nota al riordinamento*, Trani 1895.
1899
Spinazzola, V., *La R. Pinacoteca del Museo Nazionale di Napoli. Secondo contributo al riordinamento (1815-1870)*, Trani 1899.
1900
Morelli, M., *La Pinacoteca del Museo Nazionale*, in Napoli d'oggi, Napoli 1900, 95-116.
1901
Filangieri di Candida, A., *La Pinacoteca Nazionale di Napoli ed il suo riordinamento*, in «Napoli Nobilissima» X (1901), 33-35.
1902
Del Pezzo, N., *Siti reali. Capodimonte*,

in «Napoli Nobilissima» XI (1902), 65-67, 170-173, 188-192.
Filangieri di Candida, A., *La Galleria Nazionale di Napoli (Documenti e ricerche), in Le Gallerie Nazionali Italiane*, Roma 1902, vol. V, 208-354.
1905
Bernabei, F., *Relazione d'inchiesta sulla Pinacoteca di Napoli*, in «Rassegna d'arte» V (1905), 78-79.
1906
Dalbono, E., *Relazione sul riordinamento della Pinacoteca di Napoli letta alla R. Accademia di Archeologia, Lettere e Belle Arti*, Napoli 1906.
1908
Bartolotta, S., *La Galleria Nazionale di Napoli e il suo riordinamento*, estratto da «La Scintilla» 1908, 229-272.
1910
Dalbono, E., *A proposito di alcuni mutamenti nella R. Pinacoteca di Napoli*, Napoli 1910.
1911
De Rinaldis, A., *Museo Nazionale di Napoli. Pinacoteca*. Napoli 1911.
1928
De Rinaldis, A., *Pinacoteca del Museo Nazionale di Napoli*, new edition, Napoli 1928.
1932
Quintavalle, A.O., *La Pinacoteca del Museo Nazionale di Napoli*, Roma 1932.
1948
Molajoli, B., *Musei e opere d'arte attraverso la guerra*, Napoli 1948.
1951
Molajoli, B., *Note illustrative del progetto di sistemazione del Museo e Gallerie Nazionali di Capodimonte*, Napoli 1951.
1953
Molajoli, B., *Opere d'arte del Banco di Napoli*, Napoli 1953.
1956
Hayward, J.F., *Les collections du Palais de Capodimonte à Naples*, in «Armes anciennes» I (1956), 121-140, 147-163.
1957
Molajoli, B., *Museo e Gallerie Nazionali*

di Capodimonte. La donazione Alfonso Marino, Napoli 1957.
Molajoli, B., *Notizie su Capodimonte*, Napoli 1957.
1958
Ferrari, O.-Stazio, A., *La donazione Mario De Ciccio*, Napoli 1958.
1959
Molajoli, B., *Ritratti a Capodimonte*, Torino 1959.
1961
Molajoli, B., *Il Museo di Capodimonte*, Cava dei Tirreni 1961.
1962
Causa, R., *La Sala Toma*, Napoli 1962.
1966
La Reggia di Capodimonte, edited by Gino Doria and Raffaello Causa, Firenze 1966.
1972
Napoli: *La collezione di Angelo Astarita al Museo di Capodimonte*, a cura di Nicola Spinosa, Napoli 1972.
1975
Napoli: *Acquisizioni 1960-1975*, Napoli 1975.
1982
Le Collezioni del Museo di Capodimonte, edited by Raffaello Causa, Milano 1982.
Tiberia, V., *Il «Museo Sacro» del Cardinale Borgia a Capodimonte*, Napoli 1982.
1984
Il Patrimonio artistico del Banco di Napoli, Napoli 1984.
1987
Bertini, G., *La Galleria del Duca di Parma. Storia di una collezione*, Milano 1987.
Muzii, R., *I grandi disegni italiani nella collezione del Museo di Capodimonte a Napoli*, Milano 1987.
1992
Spinosa, N., *Musei e raccolte storiche a Napoli*, in «Il Museo» I (1992), O, 77-80.
1993
Utili M., Leone de Castris P., Spinosa N., *Capodimonte, da raccolta storica a Galleria Nazionale. Realtà e progetti*, in «Il Museo» 1993, 1-2, 1-26.

Index of Artists

Index of Factories

Published by Electa Napoli
in June 2003

Typeset by Photocomp 2000, Napoli
Photolithos by SAMA, Quarto, Napoli
Photo-engraving by Cooperativa Nuovo DMS, Napoli
Printed by Incisivo, Salerno
Bound by Legatoria S. Tonti, Mugnano, Napoli